Sleeping With The Enemy

My Fight Against A Spiritual Assassin

By

Doreen Saunders

Table of Contents

Dedication

I dedicate this book to God the Father, Jesus my Lord and Savior and to the precious Holy Spirit. I am so grateful that I was chosen to go through this test and the grace to pass the test. You revealed to me that you are my heavenly Father and nothing could separate me from Your love. Your love reached down from heaven and delivered me from the grips of going to an eternal Hell. I pray that this work will edify the Body of Christ and bring deliverance to those that are blind and bound by the grips of Satan. My prayer is that I continue my journey strong and obedient to the end and to be found worthy to partake of my heavenly inheritance.
In Your Service
Your daughter

Acknowledgements

I want to give a very special thank you to the family and friends that supported me with getting this book completed. It was at times a frustrating experience and your kind words and nudges of confidence were needed and so appreciated. Thank you!

To my beloved children,
I love you and want you to know that your faith in the God in me means more to me than you will ever know. The best is yet to come!

Introduction

First, let me ask you this question; *Do you believe that there is a natural and a spiritual realm of existence?* Well whether you believe it or not there is and that spiritual realm cannot be seen with your twenty-twenty vision. Much of what I will be sharing was first revealed to me through dreams and visions before this encounter occurred. I am sharing my testimony of a battle with a demonic spirit whose assignment was to destroy my destiny. This encounter resulted in me going through spiritual attacks on my mind that were so evil that the Lord would have to deliver me, and He did just that.

I have heard it said by many Christians that when you get to a "new spiritual level, there will be a new devil at that level waiting to test you". I learned after going through this relationship that this was a true statement and not just a cliché. I encountered a demonic spirit whose sole purpose was to destroy my destiny.

John 10:10 (KJV)
10 The thief cometh not, but for to steal, and to kill, and to **destroy**:

Oh, and let me not forget to mention that this demonic spirit was embodied inside the frame of a handsome and fine man. In the chapter "A Slave to Pain" you will get a glimpse of how this bondage took place and how the enemy orchestrated to take out his devious plan against my life.

After having sex with this man a gateway portal was opened into my soul that connected our souls as one. I had given the enemy of my soul full access into my life. Soul ties bind you as one!

1 Corinthians 6:16 (KJV)
What? know ye not that he which is joined to an harlot is one body? for two, saith he, shall be one flesh.

This was a time in my life when I was spiritually lazy and due to that my mind wandered into fantasy. The fantasy caused me to acquire a desire for companionship. Behind my desire for companionship was hiding the spirit of loneliness. All Satan needs is a crack in your spiritual door that will give him access into your life, loneliness was the way for him to get access to my mind and create havoc any way he could.

Being naïve didn't help either and because of that I had made a big mistake. The unfortunate thing about mistakes is that you don't realize it's a mistake until after you've made it. This relationship was a big mistake! It would be one of those tough life lessons that we all go through. It would just be my turn. I forfeited blessings because I was living in sin. Sin will cost you, no matter how good it feels.

Galatians 6:7-8 (KJV)
7 Be not deceived, God is not mocked: for whatsoever a man soweth, that shall he also reap. 8 For he that soweth to his flesh shall of the flesh reap corruption; but he that soweth to the Spirit shall of the Spirit reap life everlasting.

After I had been in the relationship for a period of time the smoke screen began to clear. I began to realize that I was losing my spiritual identity. Even more so the man that I was deeply in love with had nothing in common with the God that I love. He was an instrument that Satan was using to prepare me for something that I never anticipated, spiritual destruction. I was in love with this man! How could this turn out like this?

My spiritual walk was altered as I was becoming comfortable in darkness and with dark things. It was then that I was headed for the final stage of literally becoming a walking dead woman. My life was being depleted one layer at a time, and because of that depletion spiritually I was dying.

My purpose for writing this book is two-fold. The first reason is that just as I had initially thought, many people don't realize that they are in a spiritual battle because they cannot discern the <u>spiritual attacker</u> from the physical person.

<u>Ephesians 6:12 (KJV)</u>
12 For we wrestle not against flesh and blood, but against principalities, against powers, against the rulers of the darkness of this world, against spiritual wickedness in high places.

We tend to gravitate our reasoning towards what we can naturally see. Because of this we don't spiritually discern the identity of who is really attacking our life. Let me put up a balloon note right that not every person that you have been in a relationship with now or even in the past may have been under a demonic influence. I don't want you to confront people like they are walking around with demons in them, some may be. Just use wisdom. The second reason I am writing this book is to give my testimony on how I got free from this diabolical spiritual attack.

I first had to want my spiritual freedom then make the decision to accept God's will. I'm thankful every day that I did. Living a worldly life had taken me to a dark place. My sincere prayer is that if you have had or are having relationship issues that you allow the Lord to direct you in making decisions regarding who you allow to be attached to your 0life.

Please pray this prayer with me;

Heavenly Father in the name of Jesus I ask for a release of Your anointing power to break every chain of bondage that the enemy has over the lives of your people. Open every blind eye and deaf ear so that they can clearly see and discern the devices and snares that have been executed to ensnare lives. Grant them the spiritual vision to see what is true in every dark and hidden situation. Release your angels of protection to war against the evil that has surrounded or attached itself to the lives of each person reading this book. Father allow your healing rain to fall from heaven to heal their wounded souls. I ask that as they read this book they receive divine revelation concerning not just their relationships, but their life situations. I bind every spirit of discouragement and despair and I decree and declare that you will live again, you shall come out of this situation. Father in Jesus name I plead the blood of Jesus over their lives of every person reading this book. I ask that you surround them with a wall of protection even now, in Jesus name I pray, Amen.

Let me share my testimony of how I was delivered from my bout of *"Sleeping With The Enemy, My Battle Against A Spiritual Assassin[1]"*. Walk with me...

---

[1]   An **assassin** is someone who murders an important political or religious/spiritual leader.

CHAPTER I

Pay Attention To The Warning Signs!

Proverbs 16:18
Pride goes before destruction, And a haughty spirit before stumbling.

Where do I start with this, well I believe the beginning is a good place to start with the summary of what happened with this encounter. Approximately two years prior to when this relationship began, I had made a life changing decision to relocate from New Jersey to Georgia being led of the Lord to relocate to Georgia. I had great anticipation for what God had in store for me because of this transition.

This would be the first time in my life that I would make a decision like this, or even live alone. It would be a new beginning; and a fresh start. Because of this drastic change I was filled with an enormous feeling of excitement. This would be first time in my life I would be doing something I had never done!

You know how a kid feels in a candy store right, excited! They want everything sweet they see. That's how I felt! I just knew that everything in my life was going to be nice and sweet. Meaning it had to be all good things in store for me, right? However, after my first six months in Georgia, I began to realize that it wasn't going to be as sweet as I had thought it would be. I was not prepared for the personal challenges that would be a part of my transition.

One of my biggest challenges was of me having to adjust to living alone. This was a struggle for me because I come from a large family and I am acquainted with having a lot of people in and around my life. I had not until ths time in my life been completely alone. In crept the feelings of loneliness because I didn't know how to handle those emotions. Leaving my home to go to work and coming back home with no one else there was just something that I wasn't accustomed to. This would be my personal struggle and I was having a hard time trying to adjust to this change.

I would frequently journey back to New Jersey, almost every two months. When there I would give an outwardly facial expression that everything was okay with me, and that I was so blessed to be in Georgia. However, on the inside, my heart was breaking into pieces because I missed my children and family so much. Almost every trip back from New Jersey was of me driving home with my eyes being filled with tears. This is too much for me to deal with Lord! Why am I here? These were some of my personal shouting matches I had with the Lord.

The Lord would console my heart and tell me that my destiny was tied to me being Georgia, but I wasn't interested in hearing what He had to say to me. I wanted to go home. Even though I was upset about this transition, I knew in my heart that I would still obey the Lord. He instructed me to come here so I would just have to walk this situation out. This would be a wilderness experience for me, and I had no idea how I would overcome my struggles. I tried reading the bible, but the feeling of loneliness caused me to slip more and more away from God. This is when I began to entertain thoughts of getting me a man.

The loneliness I was feeling was the opening that Satan needed to enter into my life. He didn't have to force his way in, I let him in. The Holy Spirit would speak to my heart and tell me not to go on these dating websites, but I didn't listen. I felt like I was only looking what could be the harm in that? Every prompting or warning I received I ignored. Because I ignored those warnings, I would have to go through the test.

Prior to me even going through the relationship, I received warning signs that came through dreams and visions. I received these dreams and visions about two years before the relationship began. At the time that I received those dreams and visions I didn't realize they were warnings. I wasn't in a relationship, so what could these dreams and visions be about? As you may have figured out by now, I did not heed those warnings, neither did I believe that they would be of any serious threat to me. I'm sure now that if I had I would be writing a different testimony. Warnings can be revealed to us in many forms, dreams; visions; a gut feeling or they can come from another person that the Lord has revealed something to concerning our lives.

I believe that what can sometimes be challenging is determining whether a warning we have received is really a warning or just a bad thought or dream that we have had. Maybe I had that dream because of something that I ate last night? We sometimes try to rationalize why we have had a particular dream or vision at least that is what I did. The key to getting a revelation to what has been shown to you is to seek God concerning the matter.

You might also think that the Lord is showing you something about someone else, and that might be the case just seek Him to get the deeper revelation? I assumed what I was shown was about someone else, so I said a brief prayer and that settled the matter for me. It never came into my mind that I might just need to pay closer attention to what was being shown to me.

Let me share with you a couple of the warning signs I had received that were specifically shown to me regarding this relationship. One of my first warnings came through a dream.

A Dream

In my recount of what I believe was one of the first warnings I received was a dream of me riding in a red convertible car with a handsome gentleman. We appeared to be happy as he drove us to a boardwalk. This boardwalk was wide enough for him to drive on. He drove us close to the edge of the boardwalk and parked. I remember looking around to see where we were and noticed that the boardwalk was surrounded by a large ocean. The water was a beautiful crystal blue. The view was so beautiful and peaceful. I also noticed that we were the only ones there.

I felt so happy as I glanced over at him smiling as we sat in his car talking. At some point during our conversation, it seemed to get a bit heated and we started to argue or have some sort of disagreement. I started to make an attempt to get out of his car, I just felt like I wanted to get away from him. He very forcefully grabbed my hands to stop me and we started struggling because he did not want me to leave. At some point during our struggle, he handcuffed both of my hands to the steering wheel. I was bewildered as I thought to myself where did he get those handcuffs from?

I now had this wide-eyed puzzled look on my face because not only did I have on handcuffs, but he was no longer in the car with me! He had vanished! I was now in this car alone, and to make matters even worse the car started moving, and it was headed directly towards the ocean with me inside. I was terrified!

At this time, I became fearfully aware of the fact that the car I was in was going to plunge into the ocean with me handcuffed to the steering wheel! I was frantically trying to get out of the handcuffs, to no avail. The car drove over the edge of the boardwalk and began to sink into the ocean until I was fully submerged. I noticed that the water started to get darker and darker as I was sinking further into the depths of the ocean.

The light above me was diminishing and it looked pitch black below me. I cannot tell you how I finally got free from that steering wheel, but I did. It had to be divine intervention that broke me free. I never saw what or who it was that removed the handcuffs, they just popped off and I was free. Once I was free, I started swimming as hard as I could towards the oceans' surface with my arms stretched out in front of me. I remember having this thought as I swam, "I hope I have enough air to reach the top."

I could see the sun light above me shinning on the surface of the water. I swam towards the surface as if my life depended on it! It was at this point that I awoke from the dream. I pondered and thought about this dream as it puzzled me. The dream was so vivid and clear, what could this dream be about? I didn't have a good feeling about this dream at all. *Why? Because I never saw that I had reached the top.*

I didn't want to share this dream with too many people because I wasn't sure what it meant and I didn't feel like it was going to have a good outcome, whether it was concerning me or someone else. I eventually talked to a couple of people about it, but I left it alone once they didn't have an answer either. I had this dream about two years prior to this relationship. Can you say out loud, *that was a warning*!

A Vision

I received another warning that came through a vision. It actually started happening while I was on the phone talking with a close friend. As we talked I started feeling extremely sleepy. The sleepiness came on me suddenly, almost like I was induced with anesthesia. It was a strange feeling because I had just awakened from a good nights' rest. I told my friend that I was going to take a nap because I was feeling extremely tired. As soon as I hung up the phone I literally went right into a deep sleep. I'm talking about within seconds!

Once asleep I realized that this was not a natural sleep but the Spirit of God was trying to reveal something to me that I could only see in the realm of the spirit. Once my spiritual eyes were opened to the spirit realm I could see that I was still in my bedroom. I saw a picture in my mind of a white door with a small speck of red paint on it. I don't believe that this door was the door to my bedroom. I believe it was something that was a part of the revelation that the Lord wanted to show me.

I remember having this thought regarding the door I saw in the vision, "Why didn't they paint the entire door red, instead of this one small speck of red?" It didn't make sense to me, and as quick as I had the thought I let it go as if it was a fleeting thought. Trust me everything in this vision had a meaning! The vision then transitioned to where I saw myself lying on my bed facing my bedroom door. I was lying in the same position I was in when I fell into this deep sleep. The only difference was that in the spiritual realm I couldn't move. I tried moving to the right and to the left but I couldn't move at all. I remember feeling afraid because I didn't understand what was happening!

Since I couldn't move my body I started looking around the room as much as I could with my eyes. I started calling on the Lord Jesus to help me because I knew something was going on here. When we get into trouble we will call on Jesus for help. I could not turn my head to see behind me because of what felt like an invisible force holding me so I looked towards the foot of my bed.

As I looked down at my feet I saw that something was behind me and it looked like the leg of a large furry animal similar to a bear. I could only see the fur on its leg, it looked black and the fur was moving. I sensed that it was evil and I began to frantically call on the name of Jesus even more. I don't believe I was supposed to see further as it might have shaken me up even more than I already was.

Now just as quickly as I went into this vision I was awakened to the natural realm and I was bewildered! I remember saying to myself, "What was that all about?" I immediately began *binding and casting* down that vision but trust me I was a shaken woman. Why? For one, I knew that this was something that God wanted to reveal to me; and two I didn't have a clue as to what this vision meant until a few months prior to the Lord leading me to write this book.

Matthew 16:19 (KJV)
19 And I will give unto thee the keys of the kingdom of heaven: and whatsoever thou
shalt **bind on earth** shall be bound in heaven: and whatsoever thou shalt loose **on earth** shall be loosed in heaven.

2 Corinthians 10:5 (KJV)
5 **Casting** down imaginations, and every high thing that exalteth itself against the knowledge of God, and bringing into captivity every thought to the obedience of Christ;

A major lesson I learned is this; when the Lord reveals anything to you through a dream or vision, write them down and pay close attention to even the smallest details of the things you see in them. Revelations can sometimes come like pieces of a puzzle. These revelations can be fragmented as you may see one thing in a vision and another thing in a dream. Pray fervently and ask for revelation to the promptings you are receiving from the Lord. Again, write them down!

There will be some dreams and visions that you will have to fast and pray to get a revelation regarding what has been shown to you. Please don't take it lightly. Your life could depend upon it!

We have this instinct that is on the inside of us. Some call it a gut feeling that we sometimes feel when something just doesn't feel right. If we would just pay attention to those uneasy feelings or urges, we would be protected from many of the dangerous traps that Satan has planned or is planning against our lives. The Holy Spirit will reveal the truth to you. It's up to you to pay attention to them.

John 16:13 (KJV)
[13]Howbeit when he, the Spirit of truth, is come, he will guide you into all truth: for he shall not speak of himself; but whatsoever he shall hear, that shall he speak: **and he will shew you things to come.**

These were just a couple of warnings that I had received from the Lord. Trust me there were more. Unfortunately, I didn't seek God for revelation regarding what He wanted to reveal to me through my dreams and visions. Satan was planning a trap for me that he conspired to even take my soul. But the Almighty God of Glory had a counter plan to derail the enemies plan to take me from this world.

I believe that if you have purchased this book and you read these pages, God will begin to unfold the deception that has taken a grip on your life. Trust me I didn't see it coming and by the time I did I had so much venomous poison in my soul that "only" God could deliver me and He did just that.

What we have to realize is that there is a fierce and devious foe that desires to destroy us. Not just in this natural realm of existence but in the spiritual eternal realm as well. Our desires are tested daily as this is a purifying process to get us cleansed from the filth and carnality of this world. I was so naive and clueless because, for one, I had gotten off my spiritual post of praying and fasting and daily meditation in the Word of God.

This is a must as a child of God. It's the solidifying factor for us to walk and live the life that we are destined to live God's way. When you don't do the things that you are instructed to do in living a Godly life you become a bulls-eye target for Satan. As the layers of your spiritual guard, your amour becomes weakened he builds a plan of attack to conquer and overtake you.

1 John 10:10 (KJV)
The thief cometh not, but for to steal, and to kill, and to destroy: I am come that they might have life, and that they might have it more abundantly.

Satan wanted to destroy my life. If I had continued down that path of wayward filth I would have received a one-way ticket stamped destination Hell! He gets satisfaction when a fallen servant of the Lord succumbs to sin and goes to Hell. Realize that you are dealing with a real foe whose intentions are demonic and devious beyond your wildest imagination. Satan has been here a long time and has an archived file room with a folder with your name on it.

In those files are strategies of attacks that Satan has used that have worked; things that didn't work; along with things that "almost" worked against you. He has had this file on you all throughout your life. Our Heavenly Father also has a file and a plan for our lives.

Jeremiah 29:11 (KJV)
[11] For I know the thoughts that I think toward you, saith the Lord, thoughts of peace, and not of evil, to give you an expected end.

We have to make the decision to follow God's plan. You can't fight this battle on your own. Many of our problems are because we have made a wrong decision at some point in our life. Exalting ourselves above wisdom is a component of pride.

Proverbs 16:18 (KJV)
[18]Pride goes before destruction, And a haughty spirit before stumbling.

Pride is self-centered and will lead to destruction. We have to live with our choices, the good the bad and the ugly. I made a wrong choice that led me down a path of destruction. I believe as I did we all will have to make a determined decision to follow a path that will not compromise the life that you outwardly are living. You can live a Godly, holy life. It's all about choices. I didn't choose correctly and this resulted in me *"Sleeping with The Enemy"*. This encounter didn't start off all bad, in the beginning, it was the *"Start of Something Wonderful"*.

CHAPTER II

The Start of Something Wonderful

Ecclesiastes 3:1 (KJV)

¹ To everything there is a season and a time to every purpose under the heaven:

As I reflect back on this season of my life, I can remember it being a time of me finally feeling settled and content with my transition to Georgia. The Summer was coming to a close and my beautiful granddaughter was getting ready to return home and start the fall school session. I had a little sadness because I knew that I was going to miss her. I had spent several summers with her which made me feel like I had started parenting all over again, and I actually really didn't mind it at all. I enjoyed watching cartoons with her and I can't forget about the times we went to the park, but grandma was not getting on those monkey bars! No Way!

After she went home, I can remember entertaining the thought of being in a relationship. That shouldn't be too hard to do, right? One night I saw a commercial on television promoting a dating site where you could meet the person of your dreams! If my dream man was on that sight then I needed to go online and check things out for myself. After I had spent a little time viewing profiles I decided that I would create my own profile just to see what happens.

At first you can view profiles before you join, so that's what I did. A lot of the profiles were filled with fluff, meaning half of what many of them wrote about themselves wasn't true. I did, however, like to read the profiles, but mostly I liked looking at the pictures. I have to admit that there were some handsome gentlemen on that website. You could tell the ones that were intelligent as they would give you a profile overview of themselves that was very descriptive of who they possibly were. I'm attracted to a man that is well-versed and intelligent.

I noticed that after I added some pictures to my profile I started to receive messages from men that had interest in me. I quickly learned that I couldn't read any messages until I became a paid member. You can look all you want, but if you want to play, you have got to pay.

Some of the conversations I had first started with me chatting online only. That way I could do my own personal filter and block someone if they seemed to be crazy. If I felt good with our conversation I would them give them my number if they asked for it. I was careful never to offer my number first, I felt that by offering my number first I might appear to be desperate. Even after the initial filter, I might have to block a person who had underlying issues that I did initially see, or they started acting crazy! They were the kind of issues that make you raise one eyebrow.

Here are some of the 'red' flags that I noticed in my conversations; a person was quick to get angry; used profanity in every sentence; or just over the top foolish conversations; asking me to send them a sexy photo of myself. Block! After I had several conversations with a few gentlemen, and a couple of meet and greets things didn't go as I had thought, I became a bit discouraged. What I found out from the majority of the conversations was that these men were looking to have sex, and not really interested in getting to know me.

I wanted to meet someone that would grab my attention, but I also wanted this man to be a Christian. I would continue to go online off and on, but not as frequently as I had when I first signed up on that dating site. Then out of nowhere I received an email from someone that grabbed my attention! We emailed each other for a while, then we exchanged numbers and began to talk almost on a daily basis. I was so impressed with his intellect and how we would have great conversations that challenged my thinking.

He also kept our conversations centered on God, so that was a plus for me. That attribute alone made him more attractive to me. He made me feel like I was the best thing in the world that could have crossed his path and that he was the best thing in a man that I would ever find.

The really interesting thing about it was that even with us only having conversations, I was definitely interested in the possibility of him being the new love in my life. After talking for about a week we decided to do our meet and greet. I was like when and where baby! Meet-and-Greets can be fun! I was definitely excited about meeting him and I really hoped that he would look like his pictures. I knew if he did I would be pleased. In his photos he was handsome!

I had already had a couple of meets and greets where the person I met looked nothing like the photo they had on the website. You have to be careful and I was hoping this wasn't going to be a *catfish* meeting, like I had had before. *(Catfish: An individual pretending to be someone else, by displaying photos of another person pictures, or showing pictures of themselves when they were 20 years younger)*

I met one guy who told me he had been catfished by a *63-year-old woman*, pretending to be a *30-year-old* woman. He said she wasn't attractive at all. She was pretending to be someone else in hopes of finding a man to love her. I really didn't want to have that type of encounter.

Unfortunately, with him there was no chemistry, even though for a while we still continued to talk on the phone here and there, but there were no sparks that ignited us to go any further than having a friendship. It' can be like that sometimes, I just don't believe we have to settle for being with someone that you are not interested in. That's not fair to either of you.

Now let me get back to the guy I was interested in. The day we met, the weather was absolutely beautiful. It was sunny and a little breezy outside. Seemed like such a nice day to meet a new potential love interest. We had exchanged photos through our phones, so we each knew what the other looked like and I believe we both shared a mutual attraction to one another. At this point, I could say that I was smitten by him just from our conversations and his appearance.

Our first meeting was at a diner. I had gotten to the restaurant around 4 o'clock and he was already eating. As I walked in our eyes met and at that moment I was so taken by him that I just melted inside and exuded a big smile on my face to let him know I was in approval of our first meeting.

He asked me if I wanted to share some of his food, but I was too nervous to eat anything so I declined. The attraction between us seemed to be irresistible and I was sure he felt what I was feeling as well because he had that same smile on his face. We left the diner and went and sat in my car after he had eaten. We started listening to a radio station that played R&B which set the atmosphere for love. We talked; laughed and listened to music until well after 9 o'clock in the evening then we both went home.

I was so smitten that I recall feeling like I didn't want to leave his presence, and this was the first meeting! I felt like I had just met my amazon king. His features were unique and his frame was masculine and he was over six feet tall. He had the look similar to Morris Chestnut in the movie "Best Man".

He had such a way with words that was not at all sexual but sensual and engaging. He was also charming and his way of talking with you would make you feel relaxed and comforted. He seemed to always speak with subtle grandeur, such as "I understand and guess what, I am the one you need to handle all of that"; "I am your King; you just don't know it yet". We would have these wonderful conversations that sometimes lasted for hours and that was so refreshing because I liked to talk (smiling). I felt like this was the *start of something wonderful.*

I didn't talk to him again until the next morning. I could hardly wait as this man "had me at hello". I think you know what I mean. I would talk to him on the phone and ball up in a knot and my toes curl up. It felt like that high school kind of love where your adrenalin is flowing and you never get tired of being with or talking to that person. I couldn't stop smiling when I would see him, I had this big ole' cheesy smile on my face, you just know that I was hooked, right? I knew this was the beginning of something wonderful.

Our next meeting was about a week after our first meeting and unfortunately there had been a tragedy within his family that resulted in the loss of a loved one. Being the Christian woman that I am, I had to step in and be there to support him.

From that point on we were an item. Or as he would say I was his woman and he was my man. I would drive every weekend to see him and the drive, though far was nothing because I was so in love I didn't care one bit about the distance or time it took me to get where he was. Did I mention he could cook! He made some fried greens, cornbread in a cast iron skillet with fried chicken that would make you hurt yourself. He could make biscuits from scratch and cut up greens, oh wait, I'm getting hungry let me move on. Was I impressed, yes!

On Saturdays, we would get up early in the mornings and take a ride to the park so we could talk, or we would just go and get a cup of coffee. He liked to take pictures and I could take some really good photos of him so we would do our own little photo shoots in the park. His presence commanded attention and so did mine. Often if we went anywhere together people would say, you both make a really nice couple. We both would have big smiles on our faces from the praises of others.

On our third meeting he introduced me to his mother. She is a very observant woman who didn't have a problem speaking her truth. I liked that about her. I believe because of that that we got along very well with each other. I believe she felt the same way about me too.

So yes, this was the *start of something wonderful*. I remember clearly the first time that he came to stay the weekend with me he took me to dinner and fed me some his asparagus and mashed potatoes (Yes, I can even remember the food...lol). Ladies, you know that as women we really like when a man does this. I was trying to get my grown and sexy on by having a Margarita. Okay now knowing myself, I can hardly handle an alcoholic cooler that only has 7% alcohol, but I was trying to hang with my baby that night so I gave it a try. Oh, well the night ended well, won't talk much about that I'm going to leave that in my closet.

Those were just some of the really good times we shared together. You have to know that I nosed dived deep in love with this man and we continued on with this beautiful honeymoon experience for about six months. Then you guessed it the tables started to turn.

The start of something wonderful, or so I thought was going to be a battle in a wasteland of confusion. It would become a dry place in my life and because I didn't *"Pay attention to the warnings"*, I ended up *"Sleeping With The Enemy"*.

CHAPTER III

Sleeping With The Enemy

1 Corinthians 6:16 (KJV)

16 What? know ye not that he which is joined to a harlot is one body? for two, saith he, shall be one flesh.

Say What? Trust me no one wants to believe that the person they are in a relationship with could possibly have a connection to a demonic spirit. I know it sounds like something from a sci-fi movie, but this is a true spiritual reality. I was already deeply involved in this relationship before I realized that the man that I was involved with did not have the Spirit of God on the inside of him. His spiritual candle had either never been lit or it had completely gone out! There were two main demonic spirits that worked through him continuously to attack my life. The first one was seduction *(enticement)* and the other was manipulation *(control)*.

> *Seduction: 1: the act of SEDUCING; especially: the enticement of a person to sexual intercourse; something that attracts and charms*

The spirit of seduction was charming me with verbal lies not just of sexual persuasion by giving me an attractive view of the life that we would share together. When in actuality he had no intentions on fulfilling those charming words. They were nothing more than falsified fantasies that sounded good. I had no idea that I was under the influence of a seducing spirit. His words were so charming, but they were also calculated. He knew what I wanted so he was giving me what I requested. Satan is always listening we have to stop talking so much letting him know what we want, and he has no problem delivering it to you.

The spirit of seduction when used by the enemy can appear to be very attractive because it is disguised that way to captivate you with interest for that person that they want to use. The seductive urges that you have are not natural relational desires, they are demonically influenced causing the intent of them to be sensually persuasive to attract your desire for that person that the enemy wants to use. Initially the seduction came through his appearance and then through his strategic usage of enticing words. *Such as I will always love you. I have never loved anyone like I love you baby.* You are the women of my dreams referring to me physical appearance being his greatest desire.

He would frequently talk about our intimate encounters. This was to keep those thoughts in the forefront of my mind. These conversations kept me desiring him, however it also polluted my thoughts. I also had an intense desire to be with him even without the intimacy. I felt the temptation to just be in his presence. Weird enough that alone gave me some form of fulfillment. The spirit of seduction is truly a charmer.

The real underlying plan of seduction was to charm its way into our lives and convince us to believe that the bible was not truly the Word of God. Seducing spirits target our spirituality and once we have given in to sin, they begin work on changing what we believe. It becomes easier for you to be spiritually attacked after you have engaged in fornication, because the enemy gains access to you through the soul-tie.

The enemy's objective is to bring spiritual decline to your morality and attempts in getting you to believe that sin is okay. This man was trying to convince me that God has created us to love one another, and since God loves us, He will forgive us of our shortcomings of sin. This is a lie from the pit of Hell and it smells like smoke! This is a doctrine of devils!

1 Timothy 1:4 (KJV)
4 Now the Spirit speaketh expressly, that in the latter times some shall depart from the faith, giving heed to seducing spirits, and doctrines of devils;

I didn't recognize that it was a spiritual attack because I was so captivated by this man through the enticement of the spirit of seduction. I thought I was in love never realizing that the enemy had already infiltrated my soul. I just couldn't seem to resist him. The life lesson I learned from this was with anything in life you have to have *self-control.* We should never allow our desires to be a leading factor in our relationships.

Manipulation

Another demonic spirit is manipulation. That spirit works strategically to manipulate you to believe things that are not true. What they say sounds so close to the truth that you have to go back to the Word of God to confirm what they have said to you. Prove all things as Apostle Paul has instructed us to do. This spirit of manipulation caused me to push my life into the background and to push his life to the forefront. Manipulation is used to get you to do things for someone else, without you really knowing that this was the sole purpose of what they wanted from you. They make it appear to you as you if you are doing it of your own free will, when in fact that have been suggesting to you the very thing that you are doing for them.

> **ma·nip·u·la·tion;** 1 a. The act or practice of manipulating. b. The state of being manipulated. 2. Shrewd or devious management, especially for one's own advantage.

I would literally jump to please him and would eagerly give anything that I had in an attempt to keep things peaceful and loving in our relationship. I was manipulated to the point where it felt like I was working for him and not in the relationship as his partner. He made it seem like he wasn't trying to get anything from me by speaking one of his many lies of being disadvantaged and taken advantage of all of his life. I was actually paying and serving him to obtain his love. Looking back on that relationship, I can see that he was never looking to give, he always had the expectation to receive.

When I first met this man, he pretended to be a sold out, I love the Lord Jesus Christ kind of man. Oh, Yes, I love the Lord! However, after some time in the relationship, I began to see him differently than how I first saw him in the beginning. After a while, I wasn't the same way I was in the beginning either. I was no longer that holy sanctified woman of God that was waiting on her husband from the Lord before having sex with a man. I had indulged myself into a relationship where I was fornicating on a regular basis.

This is a devious device of the enemy. To obtain control of you to the point where you don't recognize what is being done to you. Once you see the truth you can no longer be ignorant of the enemy's devices.

2 Corinthians 2:11 (KJV)
[11] Lest Satan should get an advantage of us: for we are not ignorant of his devices.

The manipulation was subtle and targeted. He would always emphasize that he needed a good Christian woman to help him to do better in life. One thing that I had heard him say at least several times in my hearing was: *"...All I really needed in my life was to have a woman come in and help me get on my feet and lead me the way I should go."* Sounds like a job for Jesus to me! Listen, if Jesus couldn't help him to get it right, "What was I going to do"? At that time, I guess I thought I was going to be his savior. That was my foolish thinking, he needed deliverance and after a while so did I, because I had gotten myself bound too.

The excuses were so foolish that looking back on them I wish I could go back in time and smack my own self upside the head. Listen to a few of the excuses that he gave after I confronted his shortcomings; "I'm just a man"; "*We all fall short, that's why God gives us grace*"; "Nobody's perfect"; "*God will forgive us, all we have to do is repent*". All of these excuses were used to enable him to manipulate me and if I was going to be a good Christian woman I wasn't going to judge him on his faults.

The effects of the manipulation started to manifest as I allowed the enemy to use him to deter me from going to church. He would say; *You don't have to go to church to be saved! The Bible doesn't say that! Those preachers just want your money!* The enemy would get him to frequently use subtle strategic statements to get me to do, or not to do what he wanted.

The major plot of Satan was to use this man to get me to reject the Bible. *Saying it was written by man and that it is not perfect because it was written by man.* I would turn to him and give him a look like are you crazy! I believe the Bible.

The only good thing about our relationship was the sex. Even though I was going through turmoil in the relationship, I didn't want to let him go, and besides, I really did love him. It was what you might call, "my time of rolling in the deep" in dirty water. After a while, the negative manipulative words enticed me further and further away from God's truth and deeper into spiritual darkness. While the manipulation was one of the spirits used by Satan, the gateway connection was established through the soul tie that was formed from the fornication.

Souls Ties

The Holy Spirit started speaking to my heart regarding the seriousness of sexual soul ties. *Please know that soul ties bind you to that person as "one".* Yes! Whoever you are sleeping with, you become one with! Have you ever wondered why you sometimes have thoughts that are out of nowhere or you think to yourself *"why would you even think something like that"*?

1 Corinthians 6:16-18 (KJV)
16 What? know ye not that he which is joined to an harlot is one body? for two, saith he, shall be one flesh. 17 But he that is joined unto the Lord is one spirit. 18 Flee fornication.

Well, if you are connected to someone that is all over the place, you will get some all over the place thoughts too. Makes you think, doesn't it? But wait, what if there are "multiple partners"! You could be indulging with someone that has been or is in relationships with other people, and because of that you will become spiritually connected to those other people that they have been intimate with.

I've heard a few people say that after being in a relationship with a person for a long period of time that you are so connected to that person that you both begin to think alike. Why, because you are not just one in the body, but your souls are one through your intimate soul tie. Soul ties bind you as one.

Some individuals have never cut the soul ties of their past relationships so they carry whatever was connected from their past relationship into their new relationship. You can break those unholy soul ties by asking the Lord to seal up your soul from past relationships. (see *Breaking Soul Ties prayer, page 98 - 99)* The spiritual soul-ties have to be severed from the realm of the spirit.

As for me, I was an undercover sinner. Praised the Lord all through the week as the sweet church secretary. I would on occasion get to church at least a couple of Sunday's a month. I was a real pretender as I had a secret problem battling and indulging in sexual sins. Entangled in the enemy's web of deception.

I was going through my silent struggle with sin and only a couple of people that I confided in knew what I was dealing with and they consoled me as best as they could. They just didn't recognize that I was having that deep of a spiritual struggle. There are many individuals, *especially* in the church, that are compromising their spiritual walk with the Lord by secretly indulging in sexual sins. We just don't realize that those intimate connections open doorways into our soul that allow Satan access into our lives.

We see through our natural eyes and everything seems potentially good on the outside, but on the inside of a person can be a spirit that is assigned to destroy your life . We have to spiritually discern by inspecting the spiritual fruit of a person's life. That's the only way to see what's really on the inside of them.

Galatians 5:22-23 (KJV)
22But the fruit of the Spirit is love, joy, peace, longsuffering, gentleness, goodness, faith, 23Meekness, temperance: against such there is no law.

So now what? I'm sleeping with a man that has demonic spirits attached to his spirit, and now those spirits have been imparted into my soul. At this realization, I started to ask myself, why I was even allowing this to happen to me. I had even previously heard the voice of the Lord say to me, "Do you actually think I would bless you with someone that would treat you like this?"

Mind you this was after all the other times I had heard his voice and didn't listen. I had my doctor feel good and with my *naïve* Christian self, I stayed connected to him. Because "at least he made me feel good." Little did I know that the *feel bad* would totally outweigh the *feel good* and to top that off, I was on my way to Hell with gasoline panties on that were set on Hells fire.

Galatians 6:7-8 (KJV)
7 Be not deceived, God is not mocked: for whatsoever a man soweth, that shall he also reap. 8For he that soweth to his flesh shall of the flesh reap corruption; but he that soweth to the Spirit shall of the Spirit reap life everlasting.

Demonic spirits will at first camouflage their identity so that you won't recognize them inside the person. They make themselves to appear to be a good person with good intentions, but actually, they are evil and full of darkness.

Because they present themselves in a good light, or behavior you don't recognize the deceptive plan the enemy is trying to work through them. Their objective is to get connected to your soul! When you are sexually intimate it makes their connection to you easier as it will allow them access to your soul. After you become connected to them, they begin the process of affliction to ensnare you into deeper spiritual bondage.

Those demonic spirits would use this man to speak words to me that would afflict me to my soul. It was spiritual abuse. If he was in any way angry with me he would spew venomous poison from his mouth of hurtful words that seemed to cut me like a sharp knife. He was under the influence of a demon. I was paying the cost of my sin and spiritually I was dying.

Romans 6:23 (KJV)
23For the wages of sin is death; but the gift of God is eternal life through Jesus Christ our Lord.

It was not worth it. I had contaminated my soul and body for companionship and sexual pleasure. Yes, he made me feel good, but the cost was about to cost me my eternal soul into damnation if I didn't make the decision to repent and get out of this relationship.

I believe one of my issues with holding on to him was that I didn't want to feel the rejection. I had dealt with this pretty much all of my life so feeling unloved was something that I was already accustomed to. I can't blame the ones I expected to love me. I believe they were only pouring out what they had on the inside of them. Unfortunately, they didn't have much to offer me.

An even deeper revelation was that I had lost the presence of the Lord in my life. The Lord will not dwell in an unholy temple, he will depart from you like he did Saul.

1 Samuel 16:14 (KJV)
14 But the Spirit of the LORD departed from Saul, and an evil spirit from the LORD troubled him.

When you allow those evil spirits to come in and start shacking up with you, then the Spirit of the Lord *(anointing)* will lift off of your life. Trust me I know. After that Satan becomes the new landlord of your spiritual house. The more access you give Satan the more control he has over your life situations.

When I look back I realize that this was a set-up from the beginning. I was at a place where I wanted something more than I thought I had. If you fill your life with the right things, when the wrong things come your way, you won't have an appetite for them.

Matthew 5:6 (KJV)
6 Blessed are they which do hunger and thirst after righteousness: for they shall be filled.

My appetite changed after getting involved in that relationship. I wasn't on my post and didn't do the things that would have helped me to stay grounded in my walk with the Lord and the result of my spiritual decline caused me to be *"A Slave to Pain"*.

CHAPTER IV

A Slave To Pain

Isaiah 14:3 (KJV)
And it shall come to pass in the day that the LORD *shall give thee rest from thy sorrow, and from thy fear, and from the hard* **bondage** *wherein thou wast made to serve,*

At some point in the relationship I became numb to the insults, heartache and emotional pain that were being inflicted upon me. The verbal abuse had begun to happen more frequently and I would passively ignore his abusive words that were being spoken to me. I was so naïve that I felt that maybe I needed to be more patient with him and he would stop treating me this way.

I have always felt that I was a strong woman and taking a verbal blow of words was nothing new to me. If someone came at me the wrong way I would have a quick response ready to launch back at the person as a counter attack to deflect what had been said to attack me. I say this to mean that even when verbal words of attack where launched against me, I wasn't someone that allowed those words to move me.

After I became a born-again Christian I felt that I was, "supposed to forgive those that hurt me, just like God has forgiven me, right?" I was allowing this man to speak harsh words to me and felling obligated to take this treatment because I was a Christian. I wasn't using wisdom on any level with that kind of thinking and I had become, "A Slave to Pain."

Slave

[1] somebody forced to work for another: somebody who is forced to work for somebody else for no payment and is regarded as the property of that person

If I could define my visual perception during this time, I would call this my "blindsided view". I could not see what was going on because my *spiritual view* was obstructed. Having a blindsided view creates an obstruction on your blind side so that you don't see things that are there that can be potentially dangerous unless you take a better look at them. I didn't take the extra look that was necessary for me to see what was going in the relationship.

The issues were there but I was too blinded by my desire and emotions to see the things I would have been able to see if I was walking in the spirit. All the signs were there but due to my blindsided view I couldn't see them. Let me explain my definition of what my blindsided view looked like during that time:

- Picture yourself driving a car and you are in the left lane, but you want to switch over and get into the right lane. You look in your right and rearview mirrors to see if the coast is clear. After the coast *appears* to be clear you turn on your signal and proceed to move over into the right lane. What you didn't realize was that there was a car in the right lane just at the tail-end of your vehicle. Even though you looked into your rear view and side mirror you could not see the vehicle that was next to you, because the vehicle was in your blindside view.
- Many times, the other driver will honk their horn to let you know that they are there. Usually, they honk just in a nick of time warning you that you are about to sideswipe their vehicle.
- *But what if you don't hear their horn?*
- *What if their horn is broken?*
- What if your reaction time is off? What if their reaction time is off?
- What happens' next *accident!*

In our lives that is sometimes exactly what happens. We will unconsciously ignore all of the warning signs because those signs are in our blindside view. There can be a red light right in front of your face that is alerting you to stop and take a better look at a situation, but you just ignore and run the red light. I didn't pay attention to those promptings and because I didn't I would make a mistake getting involved in this relationship. I had to understand that the mirrors in my life do not only help me with how I handled past situations, but those mirrors will help me to make better future decisions in my life as well.

The example of the mirrors that we have in our lives are usually the people that are closest to us that have a greater ability to see those potential life mistakes. Those mirrors can be a family member; a close friend; a spiritual leader; or even a brother or sister in the Lord that have a genuine concern for you regarding the situation that you are involved in.

The mirrors might *see* a situation in our lives that is standing out to them like a waving red flag that has your name on it, however because you have formed an attachment with this person you just can't see it. One of the main reasons you can't see is because a soul-tie has been opened through your intimate connection with that person.

The unfortunate thing is that when someone close to you attempts to give you relationship advice on what they see requires your attention, you will sometimes ignore them. Soul-ties are deep and they bind you as one to the person you are sexually intimate with.

I Corinthians 6:16 (KJV)
16What? know ye not that he which is joined to an harlot is one body? for two, saith he, shall be one flesh.

Because you have the soul-tie attachment you will make excuses on why you feel you should stay connected to the person you are involved with. After all, when you are one with that person you don't want to go against yourself. Soul-ties are deeply rooted in you because you are attached from the soul realm. I started making excuses like, "they don't understand and besides I love this person they don't"; "they just don't want me to be happy"; "they just have to get to know him better, then they will see that he is good for me".

That soul tie just might be your next "accident" waiting to happen. Let's just hope that this is not a head-on collision that total's your car and you only have liability insurance. *Spiritual liability* causes you to have to pay a debt that was already paid for you. Because of the Spiritual liability that you obtained through *sin*, you are now an open target for the enemy of your soul that has *access granted* to attack your life.

Romans 6:23 (KJV)
23For the wages of sin is death; but the gift of God is eternal life through Jesus Christ our Lord.

You cannot expect to be blessed when you are living a sinful life. Sin brings death to the various areas of your life, spiritually, financially, physically. I got myself into this mess and I expected God to do a miracle to get me out of it. Our sinful nature will have us believing all kinds of foolishness. It wasn't like I didn't know that God is not mocked and whatsoever I sowed I would reap.

I sowed seeds of sin and when the painful harvest came I wasn't prepared to receive it. In reality what initially felt good to me, would not be something that was good for me. I should have tested the spiritual fruit of this man before I became involved with him!

Galatians 5:22-23 (KJV)
22But the fruit of the Spirit is love, joy, peace, longsuffering, gentleness, goodness, faith, 23Meekness, temperance: against such there is no law.

I've learned to listen to that inner peace that I get when something is right, more than that emotional high and good feeling that I sometimes get because something feels or sounds good. I was so desperate for affection that I ignored every rule that I have been known to live by. This python spirit was suffocating the life out of me and I was at a point in my life where I didn't even recognize myself anymore. After a year in this relationship, I was so spiritually bound by this diabolical spirit that I couldn't see which way was up down or anything else.

Emotional Prison

My thoughts were in an emotional prison and filled with continually thoughts of him. I just didn't have the strength to get out of this situation alone. I didn't want to discuss my issues with anyone else because I felt that I would be judged by them. I was already walking in condemnation on my own, I didn't need the bricks of my spiritual sisters and brothers to hit me upside the head.

On top of that I felt ashamed because I could not understand how I allowed myself to get involved in this situation or for it get to this point. Little by little I stopped doing the things that I knew would sustain me spiritually. I stopped reading my bible and my prayer life had become non-existent or should I say on the endangered species list, with me being the one in danger.

I didn't even talk to my spiritual sister much, and when I did I would just listen to what they had going on. At that time, I didn't feel like I could be of any real help because I was spiritually bound myself. I would however, always encourage to seek the Lord about their situation. Which felt was the right thing to do even though that was not what I was doing myself.

I learned so much from going through this ordeal. I knew that having discernment would enable me to spiritually identify who was the adversary that was attacking my life. In order for me to spiritually discern anything, I would have to stop sinning and get my emotions balanced so that I could get totally delivered from this ordeal.

The Holy Spirit revealed to me that the spirit attacking my life was a python spirit *(a spirit that is assigned by Satan as a destroyer or spiritual Assassin)*. This spirit would use this man to speak curses and lies over my life continually. This was to suffocate and squeeze the spiritual life out of me. As I listened to those lies they began to wear down my spirit. I started being unbalanced and unfocused. I could not maintain mental clarity for long periods of time as I was consistently thinking about what was going on in this relationship.

This began to be a wilderness experience and I was wandering around in a desert with no purpose or destination in front of me. The emotional bondage was intense and spiritually I came to know that I was under the witchcraft spirit using my thoughts to *control my mind*. Sounds like a sci-fi movie, but it's true.

I dealt with uncontrollable thoughts and suggestions that were continually running through my mind all day and night. This tool is a major tactic of the enemy to cloud a persons' thought life. Just imagine those cluttered thoughts filled with lies. When you have clouded thinking and you are emotionally unbalanced, you cannot discern when something is wrong.

Demonic spirits work overtime to send mind manipulating thoughts to keep you bound from hearing God's truth. Satan knows that if your thoughts are clear you will have the ability to discern when things in your life are off balance. We cannot be ignorant of Satan's devices. He is cunning and ancient!

I did make some weak attempts to fight back, but spiritually I was too weak due to my diminished prayer life and lack of meditating on the Word of God. My life was getting so dark. At one point I had gotten comfortable with being in a dark room because spiritually my life was dark. At times, I would say to myself out loud, "What have I gotten myself into" or "Why is this man treating me this way", I just could not understand what was happening to me.

The emotional stress began to manifest in my body. I would have chest pains and headaches along with other stress related symptoms. Your emotions can make you sick on the inside. Sometimes The emotional stress would hurt to my soul. I would cry and feel a deep groaning in my spirit because my soul was crying out to get free! I had gotten so accustomed to this man attacking me that I would prepare for the upcoming attacks. I was indeed a *"Slave To Pain"*.

I would make excuses for him because we do that when we want to justify to others "why" we allow someone to treat us badly. You have to use wisdom, because demonic spirits will use the word of God to assist them with controlling you and getting you to do what they want to do. They will speak scriptures to convince you that you have to love them; as they sow discord and havoc into your life. Use wisdom and discern every spirit to see if it is of God.

Luke 6:35 (KJV)
35 But love ye your enemies, and do good, and lend, hoping for nothing again; and your reward shall be great, and ye shall be the children of the Highest: for he is kind unto the unthankful and to the evil.

I learned after coming out of this storm that I was built to pass this test. The Father was watching over me the whole time. My Heavenly Father looked pass my sinful mess. His love is so beyond the humanistic way people say that they love you. God didn't separate from me because I was in sin, the sin separated me from God. Just like Job, this test was designed by God for me to go through. My Father had a plan to prosper my soul even with me having to go through this storm.

Romans 8:35 (KJV)
35 Who shall separate us from the love of Christ? shall tribulation, or distress, or persecution, or famine, or nakedness, or peril, or sword?

Let me get back to the blindsided view. Now there are things you can do to prevent an accident from happening. You can do a quick glance over your shoulder *(take a real look at the person's life that you are involved with)* or you can slow down and wait just a little to see if another car is on the side of you *(take your time and test the spiritual fruit of the person you are involved with; read Galatians 5:22-23)*, or speed up a little further so you can see if another vehicle is there *(sometimes you just have to flee and make no investment into a potentially messy situation, especially a situation that leads you into sin, I Corinthians 6:18)*.

I'm saying that to say this, we have to at times step back and get a better view of the situations that we willingly allow access into our lives. Abuse comes in many forms, and the most disguised form is the spiritual adversary that we can't see with our natural eyes.

Take a mental picture of where you are right now and look back at how you looked before you were involved in your current relationship. If you are looking or feeling worse in areas of your life that you weren't before the relationship. Take out the trash!

If you are being mistreated, you don't have to take that foolishness. I did because I felt that I was in love, but eventually, I had to come to my senses and realize that love doesn't hurt you. It should build your life, not deteriorate it. I was a fixer, so I thought this was another problem for "super-me" to fix or help to get better. Little did I know this was a set-up from the beginning and I was going to get a dose of his medication of pain on a regular basis.

Listen to me if you are involved with anyone that continually wounds you emotionally, spiritually and definitely physically (if physically I recommend you get your sneakers and anything else you can carry and leave) you need to take an evaluation of the relationship and decide if this is the direction you want your life to go with this person. If you can't grow, Go!

You don't have to be a slave to pain. You can live a pain-free life. I'm sure that there will be other issues and obstacles in your life, but you get to choose your battles. I have learned to fight strategically and now I fight on my knees going to my Heavenly Father and I know He hears and answers my prayers.

Because of my spiritual deterioration I had to learn to trust God again, I was in such a dark empty place of condemnation it was hard for me to feel worthy to even talk to God. If you are dealing with this type of situation, I want you to know that you can live again! You can survive this. I did. Choose life and let every destructive, empty, heavy weighing down issue in your life go!

I continued in this devastating relationship for almost three years. With the last year being off/on because the soul-tie attachment was deep and it had to be uprooted from my soul to release me from being a slave to pain.

As I walk you through my journey of going through the slavery mentality I had to overcome being spiritually crippled even deeper due to the "Torment" that I was dealing with in my mind.

CHAPTER V

Torment

1 John 4:18 (KJV)

18 There is no fear in love; but perfect love casteth out fear: because fear hath torment. He that feareth is not made perfect in love.

In this chapter, I will describe the anguish and torment I endured during my time in the relationship. My hope is that by revisiting what I went through that it will in some way help someone that may be going through a similar situation with a tormenting spirit, seek to get deliverance.

I truly desired to be in love and I felt that my biological clock was ticking and my time was running out. That was my own personal fear, and that fear was one of the reasons why I stayed in the relationship long after it should have ended.

One of the things that the enemy used against me were thoughts of my past failed relationships. I even entertained lying thoughts from the enemy that maybe God does not intend for me to be married. Especially since the Lord said that it wasn't good for man to be alone.

Genesis 2:18 (KJV)

18 And the LORD God said, It is not good that the man should be alone; I will make him an help meet for him.

The beginning stages of my torment started in my mind. I will give you just a few of the things that were said to me. He would tell me things like; "You will never be a singer"; "You won't ever be that writer"; "You are a talker and you don't finish anything". "You will always be fat, it's in your body structure". I found myself always trying to defend myself to him. It felt like I was always contending with him to hold on to the visions that I felt inspired to pursue. I would also emphasize to him who I believed God ordained me to be.

It didn't matter to him, he was just the instrument that the enemy was using to poison the visions and dreams that I had received from the Lord. Unfortunately, due to my spiritual decline, his words began to overshadow mine. I began to listen to the lies and would even ponder them in my thoughts. Sadly, it was during this time I didn't have any come-back because my spirit was in a low place and the enemy used this to attack me with every negative word that he could.

Eventually, my mind began to plummet and mesh with the words that were being spoken over my life. Even when I would try to change what I was thinking his negative thoughts would creep back into my mind. I began to feel like the words "I will never succeed" had been stamped in the center of my forehead, and I was sure that everybody else could see it. You really have to pay attention to the words that are being spoken in your hearing. Especially if those words are negatively towards you. Some words can put your mind in a spiritual prison. If your mind is in prison, your life will be too.

Proverbs 18:21 (KJV)
21Death and life are in the power of the tongue: and they that love it shall eat the fruit thereof.

Negative words can afflict; wound and dismantle your life one word at a time. When you are in love with someone, you will willingly listen to what they have to say. Sometimes you are unaware that they might be listening to the enemy to come against your life. I didn't remember that if their ears are not opened by God, they could be listening to the enemy and speaking what he gives them to say in your hearing. Their mouth can become a loaded weapon in the hands of the enemy and that gun is aimed directly at you! I encourage you to cast down everything that is not of the Lord!

2 Corinthians 10:5 (KJV)
5 Casting down imaginations, and every high thing that exalteth itself against the knowledge of God, and bringing into captivity every thought to the obedience of Christ;

If there is someone speaking negative things into your life, look them in their eyes and say:

"I don't receive that, and I cast it back to the pits of Hell, In Jesus Name!"

Don't receive any negative words or lies that are spoken against you and your destiny. You don't have to believe or receive that negative report. As soon as they are spoken to you put them in spiritual lock-up and cast them back into the pits of hell, who I'm sure is the originator of those accusations.

I can remember asking him *"Why do you speak these negative things to me? His response was; When you make me angry I attack what I love".* Okay, now this is some type of *psycho* thinking and I can't even believe that I tolerated that foolishness, but I did. I was in an emotional prison and I gave him the key to have access in and out of my mind.

Many times, these shots were subtle and sneaky things that you wouldn't normally pay attention to, such as calling you "dumb", or "you so smart you are stupid", then he would laugh about it to play it down like it was a joke, but in the back of your conscious mind you start wondering if that the really the way that feel about you.

He was the fleshly vessel that Satan used to attack my life. I was with him, but the spirits assigned to him were strategically working against me getting free. He was constantly reminding me of my past stumbles and failures always used in an attempt to offer me another dose of what I call the *time capsule of pain.*

This pill doesn't provide any physical or emotional relief for your symptoms it's just a pill to remind you of the pain that you have endured in the past. When taking a dose of the time capsule of pain (negative thinking) it will open your thoughts mentally to be right back to the place you were that thought occurred. You begin to feel the same stress and anxiety that you felt at that time in your life.

It was mental torment to continually allow my thoughts to dwell in that place. The Word of God declares that as a man thinks in his heart so is he. So, my negative internal thinking started to affect me externally. Meaning I started look like on the outside what I was going through on the inside.

Proverbs 23:7 (KJV)
For as he thinketh in his heart, so is he: Eat and drink, saith he to thee; but his heart is not with thee.

I started going through various illnesses in my body which were the effects of the torment I endured in the relationship. I would have headaches; stomach aches; back problems; hair breakage; crying spells, loss of focus; these were just some of the things that I endured. I believe when you get to this stage of oppression that the torment has taken a deep-rooted grip on your soul you will need to get spiritual deliverance.

Let me add here that my spiritual discernment and wisdom were completely disabled during this time. I didn't know what was going on with me. One thing I did realize was that "this was not what I signed up for". Yes, I desired to be with him and enjoy the psychical satisfaction that came along with that, but I was not prepared for the *"Liar"* that was on the inside of this man!

CHAPTER VI

Liar!

John 8:44 (KJV)
⁴⁴ Ye are of your father the devil, and the lusts of your father ye will do. He was a murderer from the beginning, and abode not in the truth, because there is no truth in him. When he speaketh a lie, he speaketh of his own: for he is a liar, and the father of it.

In the beginning of my relationship, I believed everything that this man told me. The reason I believed him was because I didn't feel like he had a reason to lie to me. I am a firm believer that a person is innocent until proven guilty. I already liked him for who I thought he was, but what I didn't realize was he was giving me an illusion of what he wanted me to see as a reality in his life, however that was not the case and it was quite the opposite. He wanted me to believe in the great person that he desired to be. Don't get me wrong he was a nice guy, but he just didn't speak the truth often, so I didn't know what to believe.

He was under the influence of a lying spirit that had him to speak these great big lies. That spirit used him to paint an illusion that had some truth in it, but the foundation of what he said were lies. I believe that we really want to believe what a person is telling us is the truth, unfortunately, that is not always the case. It could be because we feel that those little white lies are not so bad. Right? A lie is a lie. Doesn't matter how big or small of a lie that you tell, it is still a lie.

As time went on and the curtains of truth were pulled back I began to see that things were not "really" matching the things that I had been told. I did ask him questions about a few of the things that didn't quite match up. I would say to him, "didn't you say that this happened, and not that?". My truth- seeking questions would spark anger in him, and he would blatantly say that was not what he had initially said to me. His follow-up response would also correct me with him saying another lie to cover up the first lie. It's hard to remember a lie. The truth will stand as you have stored that truth in your memory bank and you can extract it when needed and it will still be the same.

Almost everything that he said to me was not the truth. I could share many examples of the lies that were said to me, but the main reason to bring this to light is to reveal that this is one of *the tactics that the enemy of our soul uses to manipulate us into spiritual bondage.* That person's life was the result of him allowing demonic forces to have control over his life. I was involved with someone that was in bondage to many spirits, and because I was now one with him through the spiritual soul-tie I had spirits attached to me as well.

I recall having a conversation with a close friend regarding that relationship, she tried as best she could to encourage me to pay attention to the things this man was saying and doing towards me. During some point of our conversation, *the Spirit of the Lord spoke through her and said, "In this man dwells no good thing, and he is not of me; he is of his father the devil"!*

John 8:44 (KJV)
44 Ye are of your father the devil, and the lusts of your father ye will do. He was a murderer from the beginning, and abode not in the truth, **because there is no truth in him.**

I was alarmed at what she said, but not enough to leave him. You have to remember I was connected to him intimately, so really, I wasn't trying to hear what she said because I still loved him. After our conversation ended I thought to myself, "she just doesn't want to see me happy. I finally have a man, and she has her man, why should I be alone." Fast forward to my now, *I wish I had listened.*

Emotional and intimate ties to a person can blindside you. You can only learn who a person truly is by observing how they handle life situations or struggles. Do they make wise decisions? Are they angry or calm and level headed when dealing with situations? Rushing into a relationship and giving a new person access to the inner court of your life could be a big mistake.

I am not saying that you should pull out the polygraph machine and hook them up to it and then start drilling away with questions. I do suggest that you just listen and discern their responses. Trust me you need the Spirit of God to give you revelation regarding who a person really is. It's dangerous for you not too! If by chance you notice that a persons' story keeps on changing, then look at them and say, "Either you need to get checked for Alzheimer's or you are not telling the truth!"

Not addressing these issues leaves room for the lying to continue. Of course, be tactful in how you handle this situation, but ask questions. If you deal with this in the beginning, it can help to progress your relationship and allow both of you to be honest and upfront with how you deal with difficult situations. After you have an understanding about the person you are involved with, then you can make a better decision as to whether you want to make an investment of pursuing a relationship with them or letting it go.

Demonic spirits will also try to *isolate* you from others, especially from those that can spiritually see them. One example I can reference is him **not** wanting us to attend family functions or hang out with him and his friends. He would not allow me to meet many family and friends that knew him. I believe the reason for this was because family and friends know the truth about you, and most of the time they won't lie. These can be the mirrors that reveal the true identity of a person because for some they would have known you for the majority of your life. They know the real you!

The person you are with just might not want their family or friends to slip up and reveal to you who they truly are. When a person says, "I just want to keep you to myself", ask them why? Are we going to be together and just stay in the house looking at each other? I am not addressing everything about relationship 101, just about what I encountered on my journey. *Be alert* it's about more than you having good feelings about someone!

1 Peter 5:8 (KJV)
[8] Be sober, be vigilant; because your adversary the devil, as a roaring lion, walketh about, seeking whom he may devour:

As a child of God, we are constantly targeted by the enemy to accuse us and he will do this through people. They accuse us of not really being a Christian if we try to judge them righteously. He always wants Christians to appear as carnal minded people who are nothing more than bible waving freaks, who don't really believe what is in the bible themselves. He's a liar and the father of lies. We have to walk in God's truth so that our spiritual identity is not distorted or includes the lies of Satan.

I believe that in hell, Satan has a file with our names on it that has information of the things that he has done that have worked against us, along with things that almost worked. Demons use devices and tricks in different ways to attempt to set us up for destruction. They want to get us off balance in our walk with the Lord and fall into Satan's pit of deception through his lies.

2 Corinthians 2:11 (KJV)

11 Lest Satan should get an advantage of us: for we are not ignorant of his devices.

The enemy of our soul doesn't want us to walk into our destinies so he will attack us many times through people who will carry out his plans against our lives. It goes unrecognized because we only see the person and not the spirit, and sometimes the person doesn't even realize that they are being used.

Ephesians 6:12 (KJV)

12 **For we wrestle not against flesh and blood,** but against principalities, against powers, against the rulers of the darkness of this world, against spiritual wickedness in high places.

Another tactic of demonic spirits is to bring you down *to its level of evil.* As the smoke cleared and I realized that this relationship was not of God, I got angry. I was frequently cursed at and it got to the point that I started cussing him out too! Sometimes I would get so angry at myself because I fell right into the enemies' trap by forgetting who was really the adversary that I was wrestling with. When we are confronted with evil we have to overcome evil with good.

Romans 12:21 (KJV)

21 Be not overcome of evil, but overcome evil with good.

We should not allow ourselves to be consumed with the poison that has been shot at us by these evil spirits. We have to put up our shield of faith and declare, "Greater is He that is within me than he that is in this world." The shield of faith will deflect the evil and it won't have power over you to hurt you.

Unfortunately, that wasn't the way I handled this situation, I grew angry and bitter towards him. This was not Godly love at all, and to make matters worse I decided to take matters into my own hands. Did I win? No! Because no matter what evil the enemy of our souls throws our way, we have been given the power to overcome it. We should always overcome evil with good. It is only through us doing good deeds that we reap coals of fire upon the head of the person that the enemy has used to reign chaos in our life.

Proverbs 25:21-22 (KJV)
21 If thine enemy be hungry, give him bread to eat; and if he be thirsty, give him water to drink: 22For thou shalt heap coals of fire upon his head, and the LORD shall reward thee.

When someone does evil to you, your display of forgiveness and mercy can deflect the evil that was orchestrated against you and can possibly open their heart to change for the better. Doing it your way will bring no glory to God, and no reward for you, it just gives you a personal sense of victory. In reality, you have won nothing, you conceded to the evil that was sent to derail your testimony. This was a spiritual battle and I couldn't get past looking at the carnal person to recognize that.

I was being mentally fragmented by hurtful words that would become seeds of doubt in my heart because I didn't immediately cast them out of my mind nor did I reject them. Whenever negative words are being spoken to you or lies said that are orchestrated to assassinate your character, immediately cast them down, and send those accusations back to the pits of hell.

2 Corinthians 10:5 (KJV)
5 Casting down imaginations, and every high thing that exalteth itself against the knowledge of God, and bringing into captivity every thought to the obedience of Christ;

You don't have to believe what a person is saying about you, but if they say it enough in your hearing then eventually it will get into your heart. Faith comes by hearing and hearing by the Word of God. Doubt comes by hearing and hearing by the enemy of your soul!

Romans 10:17 [KJV]
17 So then faith cometh by hearing, and hearing by the word of God.

The biggest lesson of all that I learned from this situation was that I missed an opportunity to minister to someone that was spiritually lost. The Lord has healed my heart and I no longer walk in condemnation for missing that opportunity to be a *true Woman of God.* I learned a serious lesson that I am now using in all relationships in my life.

Trust me it helped me. Looking back on the relationship I knew that I wanted him to give me the love that I desired, but in actuality he needed me to see him past how I saw him in the natural, I needed to discern his spiritual need. I was too blinded by my own selfish desires I couldn't spiritually give him what he needed. Let me share some spiritual nuggets that I believe will help you;

> ➢ Be patient and discern the spirit of the person you are involved with.
> ➢ Listen to what is spoken and address issues immediately so that it doesn't become an issue later.
> ➢ Don't compromise who you are. Don't give into the sexual invitation. You don't want to connect to anybody outside of marriage.
> ➢ Stay in prayer; meditate on the Word of God daily. That way when you hear something that's not right your spiritual antenna will go up and you can cast it out.

Unfortunately, some lessons you will never learn until after you go through them. As the truth was revealed to me I saw up front the deception that the enemy used to keep me bound. Unfortunately, I didn't realize that I was fighting an invisible foe that had orchestrated tactical maneuvers against me to keep me spiritually bound. This relationship had led me into a cave and even though I could have walked out of it, I couldn't because spiritually I was defeated and in bondage.

I really needed help and I expected those that were close to me to come and rescue me and get me out of this mess. My spiritual cry was, "Help I've fallen in a cave and I can't get out! I need Jesus!" That relationship caused a great deal of *"Frustration of Family & Friends."*

CHAPTER VII

Frustration of Family & Friends

I Peter 4:8 (KJV)
8 And above all things have fervent charity (love) among yourselves: for charity (love) shall cover the multitude of sins.

I believe many of us have the expectation that our family and friends will come to our rescue when we go through tough life challenges. After going through this relationship, I received a better understanding of how we can affect family and friends with the relationship issues we go through. We do an awesome job of explaining to them the one-sided view of how another person has wronged us. To top that off we have the expectation that they should come to our defense after only hearing your one-sided story. No, it's not fair, but unfortunately, that is what I expected.

Let me make an observation of the judicial system. There is a judge; prosecutor and defense lawyer. Depending on the severity of the case they may have to bring in a jury to make a final decision. The case is presented and both parties stand before the judge to present both sides of the case. They may even bring in other *witnesses* from both sides to testify before the judge and possibly a jury on what they believe to be their truth. Usually, only one side wins.

When the decision is made the judge or jury feel that this has been the best course of action for "both" parties involved in this situation. Sometimes it's not, but the matter has been settled and recorded in court records, as the FINAL decision on the matter.

It can be hard for our family and friends to come to a fair conclusion after hearing only our side of the story. They know you through your relationship history, for family from childhood and friendships usually for a span of many of years. So then comes this other person that has wounded your heart and you like the little girl or little boy that you are; want them to understand that this situation couldn't possibly be your fault. Most of the time without even hearing the whole story they take your side.

There are some that are wise and they just listen and tell you that everything will work out. Then there are those that want to do a drive by and break out some windows. Either way, they are affected because you have involved them in something that was an overload in your emotions so you want those that are close to you to bring you some comfort. I'm going to first start with family and my perception of different things I endured during the relationship that may have affected them and how I perceived them as well.

Family

One of my biggest misconceptions was that I expected my family to understand how I felt. I failed to realize that the person I was explaining my issue to was not in love with the person I was referring to, I was. It felt good for them to take my side and say, "Yes, you are right and they are wrong", but that could at any moments' notice backfire on them.

Because as soon as they start to attack the one I loved, I would most likely take to his defense! "He wasn't that bad, or don't say that about him". Trust me this can happen and it did! I had to realize that they were judging the situation from a one-sided viewpoint. They loved me, of course, they are going to see things my way. Even if I'm right we should never judge a situation after only hearing one side of it.

We make a choice to allow someone into our lives. These choices can affect our children; family and friends. Our choices should not bring bondage to others. I have even encountered family members that just didn't want to get involved and they didn't want to hear about my messy situation. They are trying to deal with and figure out their own issues. Let me remind you that this was my mess and I had gotten myself into it. Remember?

I was so captivated by my prince charming and so in love with him. He was a beautiful package on the outside, but on the inside, he was broken and hurting, dealing with deep issues and bondage that he had endured during the early years of his life. I couldn't see that from the outside, and I wasn't ready for what was on the inside of him.

Much of the frustration that my family endured was me always bringing up my relationship in every single conversation. I would never have a conversation that didn't include him. That can become tiresome and frustrating for others to hear on a daily basis. It got to the point when I called that some of them wouldn't answer the phone. Truthfully, I probably wanted to talk about something that I was going through, and they didn't want to hear it.

I don't think that they ignored me because they didn't love me. I imagine it's because they assumed that things would work out so they just didn't want to get involved. So often in relationships when we go through things with our significant other and we want to vent or to say a temporary proclamation of, "I'm done with him!" We make this statement because we are feeling some type of emotional distress with that person at that particular time. We relay that message to the ones that we want support from to signify that the situation "is completely over"!

We all know how that can be. We declare it to the mountain tops that we are just done, but in two days or less, we are back in the arms of the person that we swore to the heavens that we were never going back to again. This is one of the reasons that some family members don't want to get involved. They figure they are going to get back together anyway, and I'm not getting tangled up in their relationship mess. So, they quietly sit under an umbrella while you weather the storm.

When I first became a born-again Christian, I was on fire for the Lord and He manifested Himself outwardly in my life. The Lord would give me revelations to the Word of God; my prayers were answered sometimes almost immediately. I believe that because of how I had previously walked with the Lord that my family believed this relationship couldn't be a mistake. Unfortunately, it was a mistake; I learned a hard lesson as a result of my disobedience. Sin will cost you so much. Remember the wages of sin is death.

I am known to be a very strong woman who would stand on her own at any given moment. The difference about this situation was that the opposition was not coming from a carnal (individual) it was demonic in its nature and strength. That was the difference and so the perception from my family seeing me in such a vulnerable place in that relationship was not the normal thing to see. In fact, it wasn't a normal situation; it was dressed up like one, but the intent behind it was completely demonic.

Then came the prideful side of me not wanting to reveal that I was in bondage. You have to keep up that spiritual look, all the while spiritually you are in a spiritual prison. If I revealed what was really going on I wouldn't be as spiritual as others "thought" I was. Yes, I was concerned about what others thought about me. I was a people pleaser.

After a while of going through my spiritual distress, I didn't care what people thought or said about me. I believe this is the place I had to get to access my need to get back to God. You see I came out of a spiritual battle that was strategically set up to take my soul. But God! Then I was no longer concerned about what people thought about me. I was more concerned about how God felt about me and through Him I was set-free.

Relationships can at times be difficult. We should not expect our family to solve our relationship issues. That weight shouldn't be put on them. What would have helped me through my storm would have been a hearing ear and some wise spiritual counsel. We have to understand that some people can't handle what we might be going through. I know that my family loved me but what I needed at that time they didn't have the spiritual capacity to help me get through.

Friends

When we share our relationship issues with our friends it's because we have established a level of trust with that person. What I failed to identify was the various levels of friendship that I had, and how I shared my personal struggles with them. A true friend can be our biggest advocate. Because they have a true love and concern for you. You will have disagreements and there may be a distance between you, but you or they can pick up the phone and the conversation will continue on as if you called each other every day and never missed a beat.

Like everything in life friendships will be tested as well. I learned to identify the friendships that I had whom I could trust to release my innermost secrets; frustrations; venting sessions or anything else that was personal concerning my life. Before this relationship, I did not realize that there are different levels of friendships. Knowing this will help you to determine the extent of what you share regarding your life. There are some friends that are "**unconcerned**". They are more than willing to listen to what you have to say; however, they make a point of emphasizing how they would never put up with what you are going through.

At times, they will cut you short because they really don't care to hear about what you have to say anyway. The conversation is not about them so they really could care less about your situation. If by chance you ask them for advice, they will divert the conversation off of you and start talking about themselves.

Then there are those **"judgmental"** friends that will listen and throw the bible at you and tell you that you shouldn't cast your pearls to the swine. Or how could you do that, don't you know who you are? By the time you finished hearing what they had to say you go deeper into bondage because they make you feel like you are worse than Judas who betrayed Jesus. This type of friend made me feel like I had to keep up the smoke screen like everything was okay with me, but little did they know, I was in deep darkness.

Dealing with the **"gossiping"** friends can be a challenge because you already know that as soon as you get off the phone with them they begin to tell someone else something that you shared with them in confidence. The big cover-up for releasing the other persons' secret is they start off saying we need to pray for "Brenda", knowing that "Brenda" did not give them permission to repeat what she shared with them. Plain and simple it was a way for them to gossip. Then they proceed to tell you to not mention what the other person told them not to mention to another person. This type of friend is a talebearer.

Proverbs 11:13 (KJV)
13 A talebearer revealeth secrets: but he that is of a faithful spirit concealeth the matter.

Remember this if they are talking about somebody else's situation with you, then your situation may be the topic of discussion with someone else.

I have learned that **"faithful"** friendships are built on a strong foundation. This type of friendship is progressed over the years and built upon a foundation of true love and respect one for another. This is a person that you can confide in with anything. You don't worry about whether things that you say to them will be repeated because you won't hear it again. This is the person that you can call crazy hours of the morning or night to discuss something that is an issue because you know that they will listen to you without judgment. Value this friendship for it is a gem. A true friend will stick closer to you than sometimes even your family.

Proverbs 18:24 (KJV)
24 A man that hath friends must shew himself friendly; and there is a friend that sticketh closer than a brother.

With all relationships in life, we have to evaluate the level of access that we grant for releasing our secrets. This was a learning experience and it didn't change my love for any of my friends no matter what level of friendship that we had or have. What I needed during that time was an unbiased, non-judgmental and patient friend, that could look past my current situation. I learned that at times your friends might not be able to support or assist with your deliverance.

What I Learned

There are many things that I could have done differently, for one, I should have communicated with someone what I was going through. In order to get help regarding situations that we are going through we have to be willing to share our hurt or frustrations. I wanted to appear to be strong, so I went through this ordeal alone. Now I know that whenever I see a loved one going through challenges I pray for them and ask the Lord for wisdom to talk with them anything that He may have shown to me regarding that person. I then remain neutral by not picking a side because you can never have wise judgement from hearing a one-sided view.

As a family member or friend what I would suggest that you be sensitive to what the person is going through that you do not cover them with shame or judgment by speaking harsh words. You should tell them the truth in a spirit of love. Our life experiences prepare us to minister to others, because of our encounter with similar issues. This also taught me that it can be hard for the family not to judge a situation especially because they love you. It might even be best for you to go to someone neutral so that there is no biased opinion.

They don't know you so you can share your feelings and not hold anything back. Families can be a powerful bond and I'm thankful for mine. While there will be miscommunications, disagreements, and challenges for all families; the glue that keeps us together is that our love remains intact even after those challenges.

We should be able to share our secrets with someone who will not judge; condemn or cast us away. The majority of the time all I felt was that I was being judged or they didn't want to be bothered. I have learned a great deal from this experience. It taught me not to judge, because we don't know the story behind the story. If we listen with discernment, then we can use wisdom to give some spiritual relief which is what the person really needs.

I had to learn to be a friend without judgment and love you enough to tell you the truth even if it hurts because I want your soul to prosper.

I Peter 4:8 (KJV)
8 And above all things have fervent charity (love) among yourselves: for charity (love) shall cover the multitude of sins.

Sometimes the truth hurts, but when you hear it from someone that loves you, then you can receive it because you know it's coming from a good place. There will be times that the only thing you can offer is a listening ear and prayer and that is okay too.

The overall observation was for me to realize that my family and friends may not understand my situation as they are looking at it from a one-sided view point. I had to respect them when they didn't have a comment concerning my situation. This was a spiritual battle and I finally understood that I wasn't wrestling against flesh and blood, the person that's inflicting the assault was a demonic spirit working through the person that I loved. It was a horrible situation that I needed to be free from, I was in bondage to sin but now I have been made spiritually free.

Romans 6:22 (KJV)
22 But now being made free from sin, and become servants to God, ye have your fruit unto holiness, and the end everlasting life.

The Lord rescued me. He instructed me that I needed to walk in "holiness" for without "holiness" no man or woman can see God. After going through three years of hardship and trail, I had to make the decision whether I was to going to *"Really Let Go; Or Shall I Die In This Barren Land"*.

CHAPTER VIII

Really Letting Go...Or Shall I Die In This Barren Land

Psalm 34:22 (KJV)

22 *The Lord redeemeth the soul of his servants: and none of them that trust in him shall be **desolate**.*

It was the beginning of my third year of being in this relationship and I pondered on thoughts of why neither of us were prospering together. He seemed to have such a void and emptiness surrounding his life, and it began to surround my life as well. In my observation of his life, I noticed that anyone that had been connected to him in past relationships had dealt with that same barren and unfruitful life that I was currently experiencing with him. It was like the brook had dried up in their lives too, until after they departed from their relationship with him.

As the relationship continued to decline, I reflected on the barrenness and mundane existence that we both were experiencing staying together. *He was in misery and so was I.* The difficult part was knowing that I needed to leave and battling with my desire of wanting to stay with him. The Lord started dealing with me and giving me signs that this man would not change. We did share some beautiful times together; however, they didn't last long and were few in number.

Everything around me was starting to look like a barren wasteland. I wasn't bearing any spiritual fruit or material blessings. It got to a point where the majority of the time my life was filled with unhappiness and tears. I was emotionally and spiritually drained. I had no desire or energy to do anything. It felt like I was having my lifeforce drained out of me. I was dealing with shortness of breath and panic attacks. I needed to have life breathed back into me again. Dead things can be *places or people* that have no fruitfulness or prosperity. Everything in my life started to become barren, I had a decrease in pay, health decline just to name a couple of things that were happening to me. I was in the valley of dry bones. I really needed words of life to be spoken over me to restore my soul.

Ezekiel 37:4-5 (KJV)
4 Again he said unto me, Prophesy upon these bones, and say unto them, O ye dry bones, hear the word of the Lord. 5 Thus saith the Lord God unto these bones; behold, I will cause breath to enter into you, and ye shall live.

I knew that I had to leave, but it seemed that he had so many trials that were happening in his life that I felt obligated to stay with him. *I felt like I couldn't leave him while he was going through this, or that?* The Word of God says that we are to forbear when a person is going through trials. I was using the word ignorantly, not spiritually.

Galatians 6:1 (KJV)
1 Brethren, if a man be overtaken in a fault, ye which are spiritual, restore such an one in the spirit of meekness; considering thyself, lest thou also be tempted.

How could I apply the Word of God to this relationship when I was living my life in sin, fornicating. I wanted to be so deep and at least try to live like the Word said that I should. I wasn't using wisdom at all I needed to be free! When the Lord makes a way of escape take it and don't look back. Holding on and lingering in a bad situation can many times only make the situation worse. It was worse for me because I didn't seek God regarding it, it was all me with my desires on overload. At some point toward the end of the relationship, he started thinking that I was the problem with the negative things that were happening in his life. You see that's what Satan does, he is the accuser!

Revelation 12:10 (KJV)
10 And I heard a loud voice saying in heaven, Now is come salvation, and strength, and the kingdom of our God, and the power of his Christ: for the accuser of our brethren is cast down, which accused them before our God day and night.

I actually feel that he believed that because I was God's servant and he was with me that he was being punished by God. Every failure and struggle he was experiencing was my fault. He even said to me, "Maybe God is punishing me because of you, His servant". I believe every time he looked at me he saw a reflection of what he had not accomplished in his life. I was caught between a rock and a hard place. I knew I was going to have to walk away from him, or spiritually I would die in that barren place. I wondered why he felt that way he did towards me or how could I even be his problem. I feel that he blamed me because I was in his life during the time that these bad things were happening, so he felt I had to be the reason why things were not getting better in his life.

To put things into spiritual terms I believe that he was in his season of harvest where he was reaping a harvest of things that he had sown prior to my involvement with him. The carnal term for what he was going through was karma. It was his time to pay up for the things that he had sown in his life and I was with him when that bad harvest came. Makes you think, doesn't it?

By the end of the relationship, he talked to me like I was absolutely nothing. His words were filled with anger and even at times, I felt like he hated me. I'm reminded of one of the many times I was sitting at home crying; feeling hurt beyond anything I can imagine because I didn't understand why he treated me the way he did. No matter how much I gave or did for him, it was never enough. I would go without and it was still not enough to satisfy him. I had to constantly remind myself that I was not dealing with flesh and blood but a spirit assigned to devour and destroy everything in my life.

I was spiritually; emotionally; and physically bankrupt. I gave out so much that there was nothing left for me. You should never be the major contributor in a minor situation. This relationship added no value to my life and I actually missed out on blessings that the Lord had for me because I stayed in the relationship past the expiration date. It was long overdue to be over.

It was a barren land. Nothing to sustain me or that gave me life. The only thing that resided in that land (person) was theft, deception, and spiritual death if by chance I would have decided to stay there. I remember lying in bed and if by chance I exhausted myself even a little I would feel a pain in my chest. My heart was barely beating when I left him.

The Lord began to send prophetic words to build me up and encourage me to get out of that situation. After leaving the relationship there was still some residue from the soul attachment for a little while but eventually someone else got his attention and that was my opportunity to escape and I took it!

I Corinthians 10:13 (KJV)
13 There hath no temptation taken you but such as is common to man: but God is faithful, who will not suffer you to be tempted above that ye are able; but will with the temptation also make a way **to escape**, that ye may be able to bear it.

Surrendering my desire was the key to my deliverance. We can choose to stay in a situation and live a life that may never be successful or fruitful, or we can make the decision to choose what the Lord has destined for our lives. It's not always easy to wait and trust, but I learned through this experience that I will wait and I will trust God. I wasn't making good choices then, so the next time the Lord will choose for me. I am allowing Him to take the lead and I am more than willing to follow Him.

After the last break-up I did not become involved with him again. However, due to the intimate soul tie I still had feelings and emotions that were tied to him. Soul ties can be so deep that you can't get away without getting spiritual deliverance. Every sexual connection you engage in outside of marriage, you begin to lose a little bit more of your spiritual identity, and you take on some of the identity of the person you connect yourself too. That soul-tie has to be broken so that you don't carry them into your next relationship.

You can disconnect from the natural, but spiritually you may have to get deliverance to disconnect from the soul tie that was created through your sexual encounter with them. The Lord told me I couldn't go back and that he had severed the soul tie in the realm of the spirit. No matter how many times I desired to be with him, I realized it was finished.

You see I learned that Jesus loves me for me. I didn't have to pretend to be someone that I'm not. I could be just who I was created to be. He met me at the emptied, dry place in my life, where I didn't seem to have many friends or family to stand by me. I knew that I could talk to him and tell him exactly how I felt and he listened, no matter how low-down or dirty it was I kept it real with him. There were times that I was so dismayed that I would have to tell him all about.

I Peter 5:7 (KJV)
7Casting all your care upon him; for he careth for you.

As I reflect back on that traumatic life experience I realize that freedom was a choice away all I had to do was decide to be free. The even greater decision would be that after getting my freedom from that situation I had to stand on my decision to stay free from it by not go back.

I choose not to die in that barren land, I wanted to go back home to my Fathers' house of safety, this was the place the Lord was trying to get me to come back to the whole time. So just as the prodigal son did, I made the decision to go home, by walking away. I knew it was time for this *"Prodigal Daughter to Come Home."*

CHAPTER IX

Prodigal Daughter Come Home

Luke 15:17-19 (KJV)

17 And when he came to himself, he said, How many hired servants of my father's have bread enough and to spare, and I perish with hunger!
18 I will arise and go to my father, and will say unto him, Father, I have sinned against heaven, and before thee,
19 And am no more worthy to be called thy son: make me as one of thy hired servants.

During the final stage of the relationship I felt like I was wandering in a wilderness with no *pre-existing destination.* I was feeling lost and mentally dealing with uncontrollable thoughts roaming through my mind. How did I get to this dry-barren place in my life? As I observed the lives of various family and friends they seemed to be in a wilderness themselves. Some just didn't know it. I wasn't in my right spiritual standing so I didn't feel like I was in any position to give them advice on their situation.

I was living a lukewarm life that crippled me spiritually. This also caused me to have a non-existent prayer life. I used profanity like I was a sailor, something that I was not doing when I became a born-again believer. I had a form of godliness, but I was truly denying the power of God to overcome every obstacle in my life. An even greater dimming light is that because of my sinful lifestyle my testimony became diminished because I was in spiritual bondage.

2 Timothy 3:5 (KJV)
5 Have a form of godliness, but denying the power thereof: from such turn away.

I was still going to church and working as a church secretary with everything appearing to look good on the outside, but in actuality my life was full of sin. It was easy to put up a smoke screen in front of others to make it look like I had it all together, but little did they know that behind the smoke screen I was living a sinful life. Others that are living a sinful life will not be able to discern your true spiritual condition, but, a spirit filled believer can pick you up in the spirit and discern what you are spiritually battling. Please know that people are always observing your life and so is God.

Judgmental Christians and people that are not saved will perceive you as being a hypocrite, and in reality, you are. Living a life of sin is not a testimony of the power of God being revealed in your life. You are doing a center stage performance for Satan to those that are unsaved and they don't see the reflection of the God that you say you love and serve. I was a lying wonder dressed up in godly apparel but inwardly I was full of dead men's bones.

Matthew 23:27 (KJV)
27 Woe unto you, scribes and Pharisees, hypocrites! for ye are like unto whited sepulchres, which indeed appear beautiful outward, but are within full of dead men's bones, and of all uncleanness.

We will at times make excuses for our sins, by saying that "God knows my heart" implying that God understands why we are sinning and will grant us grace and forgive our sins. The truth is that sin is sin plain and simple. No matter how sweet you try to dress it up and make it smell good; sin is a nasty smell in the nostril of our Heavenly Father. That's why we have to repent on a daily basis. So that we are cleansed from our sins.

Jeremiah 17:9-10 (KJV)
9 The heart is deceitful above all things, and desperately wicked: who can know it?
10 I the LORD search the heart, I try the reins, even to give every man according to his ways, and according to the fruit of his doings.

I knew I was far from my spiritual Father's House, as God began to draw me back, I knew that I wanted to go home. I was spiritually filthy and financially bankrupt and my emotions were all over the place. I could still at times faintly hear the Lord calling me back to Him. I would hear Him speak to my heart and tell me that He loves me.

I knew that getting reconnected to God would be far better than where I was, *and I wanted to go home.* God already knows we are going to mess up that is why He sent Jesus. We couldn't make it without the sacrifice that Jesus made on Calvary. When I finally started to get my raggedy spiritual life together I made my way back to my first love. It was also at that point that I had to overcome feelings of condemnation.

Satan kept whispering to me that I was not worthy of coming back to God. The Lord allowed me to hear a sermon preached about God's grace, how we don't even deserve it, but He gives it to us anyway. This was a lifeline message for me to begin to hope again in my salvation. The Lord revealed to me that once I confessed my sins before Him that I was forgiven, I just needed to receive His forgiveness.

1 John 1:9 (KJV)
9 If we confess our sins, he is faithful and just to forgive us our sins, and to cleanse us from all unrighteousness.

There is a lie that is being preached that once we are saved we are always saved. That has been co-joined to the grace messages that are being preached as well. This is not in alignment with the Word of God. You have to continue walking in the ways of God *until the end.* Study to the bible for yourself and ask God to reveal where you are spiritually. He truly desires for us to be saved and He has given direction on how to work out our own soul salvation.

Matthew 24:13 (KJV)
13 But he that shall endure unto the end, the same shall be saved.

We have to continue walking in faith and not going back to our old sin nature. You just can't continue walking in sin and expect to walk through the gates of heaven. The Lord by His grace will deliver you and set you free but you can't continue to stay in an unrepented life of sin. To repent means to turn away from, not to run too. Press forward!

Luke 9:62 (KJV)
62 And Jesus said unto him, no man, having put his hand to the plough, and looking back, is fit for the kingdom of God.

You have to keep your soul clean by walking in godliness and holiness before the Lord. Many in the churches today are comfortable with committing sin, because and the enemy is using the grace message to keep those bound in sin, so that they stay in their sin. Do I judge? No, because I know that before I can discredit the shackles of sin and shame off of somebody else's life, I need to deal with my own sin issues. Sin is sin deal with it and move forward.

I wanted to live a righteous life, but I had taken a detour that entangled my life into a world wind of frustration and despair. My prayer to the Lord was to help me to do better so that I can get it right. Why because I didn't want to be a Christian woman straddling the fence. I was tired of being in and out; up and down and having no spiritual stability in my life. What I needed was to be filled in my soul, because spiritually I was not prospering from my attachment in the relationship. My soul became empty, and I needed a spiritual replenishing to fill that void.

3 John 1:2 (KJV)
2 Beloved, I wish above all things that thou mayest prosper and be in health, even as thy soul prospereth.

As the Lord began to draw me back spiritually the process began gradually but I was on a steady course that was transitioning my life back towards God. When I returned home He put back on me the robe of *Righteousness*. He shielded me from attacks of the enemy when I was weak until I became spiritually strong enough to stand on my own. As I prayed and read the Word of God I got stronger.

I began to refocus my attention back towards the Lord. I got on a few prayer calls that I saw on social media. For me to be on those prayer calls at that time was a good thing. I could be neutral because no one knew me and I didn't feel like I would be judged like I felt from people that knew me. They only asked for my first name, so I felt that I could share in an environment that was safe. I didn't worry about them telling anyone, because I didn't know them anyway.

I let it all out! It was a place of safety for me, and while I knew that they didn't know me, they did, however, know God and that's what I needed. I encountered some spiritual warriors on those calls that operated in the manifested gifts of the Spirit.

When you are in bondage you don't need someone telling you that you are about to get a house or a car, you need them to give you a word that is going to get you spiritually set-free! I was on those calls long enough for the Lord to start the process of delivering and healing me through those vessels. I did however get to a point that I was always going on those prayer lines seeking a word from God instead of seeking God for myself. I want to share this part because I had become a *prophetic word junkie* at one point on those calls.

After a couple of months of calling into those prayer lines, I heard the Lord speak clearly to me and He said, *"You don't need to get on those conference calls right now, I want you to spend time with me."*

That was how I started the process of going back to my Father's House. I was broken, bankrupt and almost spiritually dead, but like the prophet Ezekiel prophesied to those dry bones God used vessels to speak into my life and they ministered to those spiritually dead things in my life. It was enough to wake up the sleeping giant on the inside of me so that I could begin the journey back home.

If you have wandered away from home and no matter what you have done or are doing. There is no better place than in the presence of the Lord. The experience that I went through strengthened me and though it was hard it allowed me to get a better understanding of God's grace that He extends to us. As long as you are on this side of the eternity you have a chance to go back and make it right and to continue fighting the good fight of faith.

The Father is waiting for you with open arms and He will lead and guide you every step of the way. The Father welcomed me back home and all the benefits that I had before were still available to me. Those same benefits will be available for you too, you just have to come back to the Father.

Luke 15:20-24 KJV
20 And he arose, and came to his father. But when he was yet a great way off, his father saw him, and had compassion, and ran, and fell on his neck, and kissed him. 21 And the son said unto him, Father, I have sinned against heaven, and in thy sight, and am no more worthy to be called thy son. 22 But the father said to his servants, Bring forth the best robe, and put it on him; and put a ring on his hand, and shoes on his feet:

I had to trust the process and know that all things are working together for my good. For a season, I was covered by the Almighty God under the shadow of his wings, being deprogrammed from the lies of Satan and restored by God's grace and truth. As I was being renewed in my faith I was finally at the place where I knew that my deliverance was knocking at my front door. *"Deliverance Comes!"*

CHAPTER X

Deliverance Comes

Psalm 44:4 (KJV)
4Thou art my King Oh God, command deliverance to thy servant Jacob.

If you happy and you know it clap your hands. If you happy and you know it clap your hands. If you are happy and you know then you face should really show it if you're happy and you know it clap your hands!

When I think of the song above it makes me smile. Reflecting back on some of my childhood memories I will at times immediately burst out in laughter at the very thought of them. However, this was not the case when I reflect back on the relationship that I was involved in. While I was in the relationship my smile was not a smile of joy or happiness but a time when I dealt with having feelings of sadness and my eyes at times were filled with tears. I didn't feel this way all the time and there were some good moments, however the bad moments totally out-weighed the good ones.

Before I got delivered from this bondage, I was spiritually in a place where I felt like giving up on walking with God. I felt so condemned that I didn't believe God was still with me because if He was with me, why was I going through such a hard struggle. I had forgotten that as a child of God I was instructed in His Word that I had to be obedient to obtain God's blessings in my life. Instead of being willing and obedient I became angry with God.

Isaiah 1:19 (KJV)
19 If ye be willing and obedient, ye shall eat the good of the land:

Angry With God

I was felling angry with God because I felt that if He loved me then he wouldn't allow me to go through such heartache, if He really loved me. Never accepting the fact that this was my choice that led me into this mess, but I was mad with God because he didn't fix it and make it right. No matter how many times I prayed in tongues or decreed and declared things about my relationship, things did not change. My fix it Jesus prayers weren't working so I decided that because God didn't fix it he didn't love me. I know it sounds crazy but this is really how I felt! I wanted what I wanted and God was not going to step in and fix it because this relationship was not in His will.

Was it foolish for me to think this way? Yes, but nevertheless that was how I felt and it would be my own personal struggle that had to be worked out between me and my Father. *I guess we all know who won that struggle!* I'm so thankful for God's love and that He looked past my mess.

Once I got myself together I realized that God loved me more than I could imagine. My prayer life became more frequent and I started feeling God's presence again, even though it wasn't like I had experienced His presence before my bondage. He ministered to my soul and revealed to me that I needed to get delivered from the soul-tie that had been opened through my intimate connection with this man. I would also need deliverance from others demonic spirits that became attached to me as well from that connection. My question to God after He spoke this to my heart was, "Lord, how do I get my spiritual deliverance from this?"

I would love to say that someone laid hands on me and I was immediately back in my rightful spiritual position having nothing that was associated to the relationship attached to me, but it didn't happen like that. It would be a process over a period of time that would enable me to have a greater understanding about deliverance and the spirit realm. God knows exactly what you need, and when you need it. He is truly always right on time!

I had to be weaned away from that spiritual soul tie like a baby being weaned from a bottle of milk. Demonic soul-ties was not something that could be dealt with through my human understanding, it's spiritual so it had to be dealt with from the spiritual realm. This battle was strategically orchestrated by Satan in an attempt to destroy the destiny that God had planned for me. As the process of deliverance began it started with a change in my thought processing. If you get free in the mind you will get free in your body.

Proverbs 23:7 (KJV)
7 For as he thinketh in his heart, **so is he**:

Breaking free

The man that I loved couldn't understand why I didn't want to continue on in the relationship. How could he understand how I felt when he didn't even realize that he was in spiritual bondage? I learned a hard lesson on trusting my feelings in some situations, I truly came to understand that everything that feels good to you, might not be good for you.

If I had trusted others that saw what I didn't see then I wouldn't have gone through this situation. I don't regret going through this struggle, because it was through this struggle that I really learned to trust God again. Now I cling to Him. I still continue to pray that God would save this man and deliver him from his spiritual bondage. That is the only way he will be able to see that he is being used by Satan to manipulate and destroy the lives of Christian women.

I had once heard a minister say something that really inspired me, she said, *"Your past should be a place of reference, not a place of residence"*. I realized that I had been set free from the relationship and the prison cell had been unlocked, but it still felt like I was imprisoned because in my thoughts I was still connected to this man. You have to make the decision to walk away from the prison. If you stay in the cell, how will you ever really be free?

Walk Away

Obtaining your spiritual freedom will at times require you to walk away from a person or a situation. I was entertaining deceptive thoughts from the enemy encouraging me to stay in the relationship, and I desired to do so in hopes that he would change. I pondered on thoughts such as, "God will save him; "The Lord hears the prayers of the righteous, He will deliver him; "As a Christian I have to show unconditional love to him". Excuses, excuses!

Even though I desired the relationship to work nothing that we tried to do would make our situation better, it was only getting worse. I knew in my heart that I would have to let go and move on, I just didn't want to deal with having another failed relationship embedded in my memory. Sometimes what we have identified as love is nothing more than a need to have another person in our lives to fill a void that we have. After one of our last conflicts I knew that this relationship was over. I just needed to walk away, this would be the only way I could ever get spiritual free.

Walking away was a big part of my deliverance and making the decision not to go back was what I had to do to stay delivered. If I entertained thoughts of going back I would quickly remind myself of the torment that I endured so that I didn't continue entertaining thoughts of going back to him. Another part of my deliverance was changing my thoughts from being negative to focusing on the positive side of everything. I had to reprogram my thoughts to do that. You have to really refocus your mind to forget the negative things of your past.

Philippians 3:13 (KJV)
13 Brethren, I count not myself to have apprehended: but this one thing I do, forgetting those things which are behind, and reaching forth unto those things which are before,

Forgiveness

Forgiveness was a major key in this process as well. I can remember the Holy Spirit prompting me to pray for the man that hurt me. I prayed for him being obedient to God, with that prayer being all of one sentence in its entirety and it sounded like this, *"Lord I pray that "John" gets saved and have your way it their life, Amen"*. Yes, this one sentence prayer that came out of obedience to God, however that prayer had no compassion or mercy for the person that I was praying for. I prayed this way because I still had unforgiveness in my heart towards him.

I can truly say that when I got to a place of praying a heartfelt prayer from a forgiving heart that my prayers were filled with tears and a God given desire for the redemption of his soul. It was this place that God brought me to where I truly felt that love covers the multitude of the sins that were done against me.

1 Peter 4:8 (KJV)
8 And above all things have fervent charity (love) among yourselves: for charity shall cover the multitude of sins.

Forgiveness was one of the main components for me to get free. Without forgiveness I would not have been able to overcome and forget all of the things that happened to me. I also found that I wasn't just holding things against him, but I had issues in my heart to resolve with other people in my life that I had not forgiven. Forgiveness freed up my soul to love and trust again.

Colossians 3:13 (KJV)
13 Forbearing one another, and forgiving one another, if any man have a quarrel against any: even as Christ forgave you, so also do ye.

I found it easier to confess my faults to others after learning that through forgiveness I would no longer be carrying the burdens of hurt or offense in my heart. At the start of me openly confessing my faults to others, it felt strange to me because I had not done this before. Some of the people that I went to seemed surprised that I was confessing my faults to them, while others would comment and say that everything was okay and that there was no need to ask for forgiveness. God revealed to me through his Word that for me to confess my faults that I would be healed and I wanted that freedom in my soul. Forgiving others unblocks your soul and removes those negative thoughts and emotions from your mind and heart.

James 5:16 (KJV)
16 Confess your faults one to another, and pray one for another, that ye may be healed. The effectual fervent prayer of a righteous man availeth much.

Loving Me!

Another part of my deliverance was learning to love myself. For a while after the relationship I went into seclusion feeling like I was dark, fat and ugly. These were words that were said in my hearing almost every time this person was angry with me. After some time of me frequently hearing those words, I began to believe those lies. I would always compare myself to others never feeling content with who I was. I found myself always going on some diet or trying to do things that would make me look great in his eyes in comparison to others. The image that I had of myself was of an unconfident, timid woman. I couldn't see a reflection of myself that was beautiful and divinely created by God.

I saw the distorted picture that Satan had this man to inscribe into my memory. I don't feel that way anymore. I had to learn to appreciate the hand that I have been dealt. Every person created is uniquely and divinely created by God. I really believe that. We may look different but we are created to look and "be" just the way we are. I love me and it took me a long time to be able to say those words and mean them.

3 John 1:2 (KJV)
2 Beloved, I wish above all things that thou mayest prosper and be in health, even as thy soul prospereth;

I started to realize that I didn't need to compare myself to anyone else, I just needed to be the best me that I could be. The Lord ministered to me and revealed who I am to Him, and that I have been divinely created to be *uniquely* me. Learning to love myself enabled me to know how to truly love others. This part of my deliverance was beautiful, because it taught me to learn about real love. I will admit that at times it was challenging for me, because I didn't have many experiences in my life where I can say that I saw what real love looked like. The visuals that I had seen all my life didn't line up with what God had shown me in His word. Actually, I had never experienced that kind of love until I gave my life to the Lord. Then He began to teach me that I needed to love him above everything else and to love my neighbors as myself.

Mark 12:30-31 [KJV]
30 And thou shalt love the Lord thy God with all thy heart, and with all thy soul, and with all thy mind, and with all thy strength: this is the first commandment. 31 And the second is like, namely this, Thou shalt love thy neighbor as thyself. There is none other commandment greater than these.

How could I love my neighbor if I didn't love myself? It seemed easier for me to do things for others, and harder for me to do things for me. I didn't have self-love, nor did I know what it was, but I would need to learn in order for me to truly love myself. Family and friends that know me, knew that I could always be found doing things for others, but for me it seemed hard for me to appreciate and do things for myself.

self-love
1. regard for one's own well-being and happiness

Sounds strange but that is something that I had to learn about myself. I had to look in the mirror and say, "Dee, you are good enough to be good to you". When you don't love you, how do you know if someone else' love is real? Such was my dilemma but I'm still learning about this and taking it one day at a time.

I finally got to a place where I was determined not to get involved again in that relationship. My thoughts were starting to clear-up and spiritually I was becoming stable in my walk with the Lord as I had rededicated my life back to Him. It wasn't easy for me to get to this place, but the Lord had a way of bringing things full circle for me and this enabled me to get back on track with my destiny. My steps were being ordered by God and he began to make the *crooked* places straight in my life. Coming out of the storm and decluttering my life had me feeling like I was on an extended vacation.

Isaiah 45:2 (KJV)
2 I will go before thee, and make the crooked places straight: I will break in pieces the gates of brass, and cut in sunder the bars of iron:

Accepting God's Will

The last part of this process was that I had to accept that the relationship was not the will of God. The Lord continued to minister to my heart and tell me that what He had for me was so much greater than anything I had ever experienced in my life, but in order to obtain it I would have to accept His will and do things His way.

While I have met other gentlemen since that relationship I never entered into another relationship that was committed or exclusive, and definitely not intimately. I am going to wait "this time" and trust God to do what He does best and that is to be the guide of my life. Trusting God's process may not always be easy, I'm not going to let you think that it is, but there is one thing that I know for sure, after getting it wrong so many other times. This time I'm going to be still and let God reveal His will to me about my destiny, and that includes my mate. Am I being super deep? You can call it whatever you want. I'm saved, single and in my process of *"Transformation"*.

CHAPTER XI

Transformation

Romans 12:2 (KJV)
2 And be not conformed to this world: but be ye transformed by the renewing of your mind, that ye may prove what is that good, and acceptable, and perfect, will of God.

The first thing that comes to mind when I think of transformation is a physical change in a persons' appearance. The revelation that I received from this experience is that you must *first* be delivered in your spirit and soul before changes are manifested in your outward appearance. At the start of my transformation I was led by the Holy Spirit to go back to the place in God when I was first born-again. I remember that when I was in that place in God I had a deep longing to be in His presence. As I rested in God's presence through prayer and the Word of God, the more my soul was being cleansed.

The Word of God clearly describes transformation as a renewing of one's mind. That is the only way for us to spiritually conform to the things of God. We must renew our minds through studying the bible. As I studied the bible I developed a hunger for the things of God. I wanted to be in the presence of God all the time. When you hunger for the Word of God it will fill you up.

Matthew 5:6 (KJV)
6 Blessed are they which do hunger and thirst after righteousness: for they shall be filled.

The Lord placed a vision in my mind of an image of a persons' head. Inside that persons' head was a person standing inside of a cage. I also saw that the person in the cage had a heavy chain that was wrapped around the top of their head, inside of the persons mind. I believe God was revealing to me that the vision of the person I was shown was of myself. He was letting me know that my mind had been placed in a spiritual prison and the enemy of my soul had the key because I was living a sinful lifestyle. Thank God for delivering me out of that bondage.

The Lord also used Ministers and Prophets to speak life into my spirit and bind the works of the devil off of my life. Once that was done, I would have to walk in holiness unto the Lord and turn away from my sins.

We all have a natural appetite whether it is for food, sex or material things, that we may feed on consistently, some of those things we feed on almost on a daily basis. Because we feed on those things we continue to have an appetite for those things. It is the same order with spiritual things, in order to change our appetite back to the things of God we have to feed our spirit with spiritual food. That spiritual food is the Word of God.

I learned that having the ungodly soul tie had taken me off track, but I also learned that God is faithful and He will restore and equip you to move forward in your destiny to fulfill His will. He was not concerned about the things that I have done. He had forgiven me, I then had to forgive myself and focus on the new things that God was doing in my life and move forward!

Philippians 4:8 (KJV)
4 Finally, brethren, whatsoever things are true, whatsoever things are honest, whatsoever things are just, whatsoever things are pure, whatsoever things are lovely, whatsoever things are of good report; if there be any virtue, and if there be any praise, think on these things.

Renewed Mind

Negative thoughts came into my mind, but I had to aggressively replace those thoughts with positive thoughts to counter attack the negative thoughts that came into my mind. I had to remember that those negative thoughts were seeds planted in my mind, that had to be uprooted from my mind and replaced with positive thoughts. You will have to cast down thoughts and imaginations to free your thinking as you replace those negative thoughts with positive life-giving thoughts.

2 Corinthians 10:5 (KJV)
5 Casting down imaginations, and every high thing that exalteth itself against the knowledge of God, and bringing into captivity every thought to the obedience of Christ;

Restoration

As the father did for the prodigal son in the bible, so the Lord did for me. I was being restored in areas of my life that had been lacking while I was in that relationship. The Father wanted me to live a prosperous life, however because there was sin in my life it stopped the blessings that the Lord had intended for me to have during that time. Yes, the Lord blesses us daily with His benefits He rains on the just as well as the unjust, but to get that overflow, tidal wave overtaking your life blessings that *Deuteronomy 28* refers to. We have to live a transformed holy life and daily strive to walk in peace with everyone.

Hebrews 12:14 (KJV)
14 Follow peace with all men, and holiness, without which no man shall see the Lord:

As my mind became transformed the Lord ministered to me regarding my need to walk in holiness. I knew personally people that are in the church that fornicate and commit adultery without any conviction for their sins. There are ministers; evangelist; and prophets that are casually fornicating and committing adultery, that are actively doing works in the ministry.

Laying hands on individuals that are seeking deliverance, yet God's servant's hands are not clean! God is not pleased with this! If you are in ministry and operating with sin in your life then you need to get deliverance from those issues and be restored. You cannot be active in ministry until your spirit is delivered from those sins, and their lives submitted back to God they should not be laying hands on anyone. Guard your soul and test the fruit of those that are in leadership over you.

Holiness

Romans 6:22 (KJV)
22 But now being made free from sin, and become servants to God, ye have your fruit unto **holiness**, and the end everlasting life.

Christians are no longer waiting until they get married before consummating their love. They want to try it out now to make sure they know what the other person is working with. Listen it is what it is. God sees and knows everything. Get your own spiritual house in order that's what I did.

After I finally stopped having sex, I had to deal with getting delivered from another sexual sin. I battled with masturbation. I didn't see a problem with it, because I wasn't with a physical person, but the Lord revealed to me that it is still sex and it opens a gateway that Satan can use to access our lives. There are also demonic spirit husbands and wives, that will try to connect to you through the sin of masturbation. Masturbation opens you up to fantasy and you will use your imagination which can connect you to the person that you are trying to get delivered from. Through masturbation I was pleasuring myself, which was still a sexual act in the eyes of God.

God is not pleased with Christians that are getting sexual play toys so that they can please themselves until God sends that man or woman along. Keep waiting, because the Lord is not going to send you His treasure that has been perfected and waiting in holiness to your masturbating on a frequent basis life. Go in the drawers and under those beds, and in those closets and throw that mess out!

The Holy Spirit led me to listen to a YouTube video by a Pastor named Derek Prince on being delivered from masturbation. After I heard that sermon I never masturbated again. He talked about spirits being in your hands provoking you to touch yourself. Well once I heard him say that, that was it for me, I didn't need to hear anything else, I was delivered. I won't dwell on it. Let's just say that God knew what I needed to hear to be free.

I felt that God had revealed that to me through this man of God, I had to resist and bind that spirit out of my hands and go to sleep. I still continued to have a strong desire to masturbate, but I had to continually resist the temptations that the devil was sending. Resisting the devil was a part of my deliverance as well.

James 4:7 (KJV)
7 Submit yourselves therefore to God. Resist the devil and he will flee from you.

We have to have a balanced life spiritually, emotionally and physically. When there are unrestricted desires that rule our lives then we are on a run-a-way train that is going nowhere. When you continue on a path with an undisciplined life that is full of lusts then you will eventually derail.

Proverbs 11:1 (KJV)
1 A false balance is abomination to the Lord: but a just weight is his delight.

I had so many cords of bondage around my life that my deliverance came one layer at a time, but I got free. It was like taking off old clothing and putting on new garments. Yes, my deliverance started in my mind and as my mind was transformed, my spiritual brightness could be seen outwardly. I was no longer overshadowed by darkness.

Proverbs 23:7 (KJV)
7 For as he thinketh in his heart, so is he.

I was being transformed from the inside out, spirit; soul; and body. This time I was being refortified because I know with an assurance that I belong to God. Your reconstruction will start to happen as your mind is being transformed into God's truth. Take out the carnal trash by getting your thought life back on track.

For a while, I stopped going to church as my life wasn't changing because the messages that were preached were about being blessed and messages on grace. I was not hearing much preaching on dealing with the sins in our lives. A tremendous part of my transformation was getting delivered from sin. We have to deal with the root issues in the Body of Christ. Get the sin out of your life. God requires "Holiness".

I am not judging anyone. I'm walking this one out myself. We all have to work out our own soul salvation and that is what I'm doing. It's personal!

Philippians 2:12 (KJV)
12 Wherefore, my beloved, as ye have always obeyed, not as in my presence only, but now much more in my absence, work out your own salvation with fear and trembling.

Iron Sharpens Iron

During that time, I wasn't connected with too many people that had a strong walk with the Lord. The Lord connected me to individuals that saw right through my mess and he would use these vessels that used the sharp edge of the sword to assist me with getting free and staying free. They were individuals that didn't cater to my flesh or my emotions. They would tell me look; "God is not in that"; "That's a trap from the Devil"; "Woman of God, the Lord has something so much better for you"; "Don't settle". I don't in any way believe that they were being mean, they had to cut through my flesh to get to my soul. That is the what I needed iron!

Proverbs 27:17 (KJV)
17 Iron sharpeneth iron; so a man sharpeneth the countenance of his friend.

They ministered to me in love, even though I didn't feel like it was love because it cut my flesh wide open. I thank God for those men and women of God. They loved me enough to see me walk into my destiny and not continue down a path that would lead me to hell. These are the iron that sharpens iron men and woman of God that we all need in our lives.

Their comments, though I felt were harsh provoked me to view my life, as I looked I didn't see the image of God being reflected through my life. I became disheartened because my life was a spiritual mess. I realized that I could no longer be content with consulting individuals in my life that would cater to my mess. I needed anointed vessels of God that could discern my spirit, see the devil in me, and cast it out! You need to get free for real! God sent those type of people in my life and they used the two-edged sword of the Word of God and I got free!

Hebrews 4:12 King James Version (KJV)
12 For the word of God is quick, and powerful, and sharper than any twoedged sword, piercing even to the dividing asunder of soul and spirit, and of the joints and marrow, and is a discerner of the thoughts and intents of the heart.

Identifying The True Adversary

The enemy uses our physical senses to camouflage himself so that he can hide and appear to us as an angel of light, but underneath that light is darkness directing you to a pit designed to ensnare your life, because Satan is a spirit but he natural forces to attack our lives. Many times he goes undetected to those that are not spiritually sensitive to discern how he attacks us through individuals that appear to be good, but inwardly they are of their father, the devil.

2 Corinthians 11:14 (KJV)
14 And no marvel; for Satan himself is transformed into an angel of light.

As my mind was renewed I started to decipher when the enemy was coming at me, even when he tried to be subtle and cunning. During my transformation process I was still contacted by the man that I loved but I intentionally limited our contact, both physically and verbally. This time away from him gave me more time to heal as God continued to pour His wisdom into my soul. We have to get to a place in God that even if Satan comes to us in the form of an angel we have the spiritual discernment to recognize his true form. We can never forget his objective is to destroy our God ordained destiny.

2 Corinthians 10:4 (KJV)
(For the weapons of our warfare are not carnal, but mighty through God to the pulling down of strong holds;)

The Lord started speaking to me about His plans for my life and encouraging me to walk into my destiny. I thank God for His thoughts towards me.

Jeremiah 29:11 (KJV)
11 For I know the thoughts that I think toward you, says the LORD, thoughts of peace and not of evil, to give you a future and a hope.

Metamorphosis

I recall as I was writing this book that I heard the Lord say the word, *"metamorphosis"*. I looked up the definition of the word and it described it as; a change into something new, or the process of maturing into an adult. This is what the Lord wanted for me to become spiritually mature. He also wanted me to know that a part of my transformation process would be that I was going to change, come to a new place in my walk with Him.

As the process of change began to evolve in my life, my desires began to change. I started living life without first stamping my dreams and visions with a no, in fear of failing to obtain them. I removed my own personal limitation of not being able to do things, and instead asked God for wisdom and direction on things first. I was being changed from the inside out. Small things made such a big difference to me, especially after walking in darkness for those three years.

My metamorphosis started internally because for years I was told things contrary to what and who God said I was. I learned that you have to get to a place where <u>you</u> believe what God has said to you about who He says you are. That's the only way you can walk into your destiny. Sure, Satan will tell you that "you are nothing"; "that you will never finish this or do that"; but guess what? Satan is a liar and always will be a liar. I made up my mind to believe who God says I am. I'm made new. Walking this thing called life out, one day at a time.

<u>Vintage</u>

When the Lord began to speak to me concerning the word "vintage", I was thinking Lord are you talking about wine? He wasn't talking about wine, He was referring to vintage in regards to being of superior quality, and even better yet He was talking about me!

Speak this out loud; "I am the top of the line, one of a kind"; "of the highest quality"; "I'm unique and there is no one else created just like me". Yes, you! God changed the image of the person that I saw on the inside of me. He wanted me to have a view of myself on how I looked through His eyes. I love the Lord so much. He's a keeper, and He truly kept me. He helped me to redefine how I saw myself by teaching me how to invest in me!

I had to learn to love myself. It's not vain, self-love will teach you how to love others as you love yourself. If I didn't love myself how could I truly love my neighbors? I evolved into a better person by evaluating where I currently was in life. Where there were deficits, the Lord filled me with understanding. I had to get to a place where the view of myself was what God said about me, not the negative things I believed about myself. I'm new and of the finest quality.

Going through that relationship cost me valuable time that I can never get back. If I can provide any advice to you I would implore you not to waste your time dealing with relational issues that are not adding to your life. Time is a commodity that once you use it, you can't get it back. Use your time wisely, don't invest in people that God only wanted you to make a deposit into. Unauthorized investments don't yield a spiritual return, it causes a deficit in your life. At least that was the case in my life. I'm still being transformed daily as I strive daily to walk in the will of my Father.

It is my hope that if possible the mistake that I went through will be averted by you reading this book. The mistakes of our past are lessons. The greatest achievement for me through this I learned some keys that may open up the mind of someone else that may be going through a similar test in life. The hardest part of going through tests, is that you will have to take that test over again. Let's get a good grade the first time we take the test.

I went through this test a few times, but this last time I learned the lesson the hard, painful way. After the last time of going through this struggle, I submitted my undisciplined will to God and decided that I would do things His way. Do I know what that entails? No, but I trust God to direct me and order my steps the way I should go. I am continually learning life lessons and dealing with other situations in life that may come up. When I got to a good place in the transformation process I could finally see *"The Conclusion"* of the matter.

CHAPTER XII

The Conclusion

Ecclesiastes 12:13 (KJV)
[13] Let us hear the conclusion of the whole matter. Fear God, and keep his commandments for this is the whole duty of man.

Finally, the conclusion! I am going to summarize what I learned from this situation and the process that it took for me to get totally delivered from this relationship experience. I would come out of one area of deliverance only to have another issue come to the surface that was associated to me being in the relationship. Deliverance can be lifelong process. Some deliverances may take time as it could be associated to things from your past, or even a generational curse. I did not understand my level of bondage, until I saw myself through the eyes of my daughter.

It would be a beautiful Summer day and my daughter would say to me, "Mommy, let's go out today". At first, I declined but she suggested that it was such a nice day and we needed to get out and just have lunch, so I decided I would go. We decided to go to one of my favorite Chinese restaurants were the food was delicious. At that time, I was feeling quite ugly inside and the outside didn't look much better either. I was always wearing dark clothing, and my outward countenance was also dark as well.

After eating lunch my daughter suggested that we go to a beauty store that was next door to the restaurant, just to see what they had in there. I didn't think anything of it, nor did I realize that it was a set-up for me until she said to me "Pick out any wig that you would like, and make sure you get real hair". She was saying to me, you are worth it, even though I didn't feel like that at that time.

As we browsed around she helped me pick out a stylish wig and I said: "But look at what it costs." She looked at me and said, "Mommy, I got you". She then told me to look in the mirror. I mean take a real look at yourself. The hard part was that I really didn't want to look at myself in the mirror because I didn't feel like myself anymore, not the Doreen that I used to know.

James 1:23-24 (KJV)
23 For if any be a hearer of the word, and not a doer, he is like unto a man beholding his natural face in a glass: 24 For he beholdeth himself, and goeth his way, and straightway forgetteth what manner of man he was.

As I looked in that mirror, what I saw was a person that I didn't recognize. I said to her, "Do I look that bad", and she answered, "Yes". I started crying right there in the beauty store, because I knew she saw what I didn't want to see, the truth! I realized that she was speaking to me and telling me the truth out of love. It was that day that my healing began. The fact that God would use her so mightily blesses me.

The beauty of it is that this mighty woman of God was given to me by God. I was always known to be a strong woman; however, my daughter saw me at one of the lowest points in my life. I was vulnerable, cast down; depressed and losing hope, not just in myself but God as well. God sent her from New Jersey during a season in my life that I needed a secure bridge to lead me back to the hope of love that I once had in God. This helped me to get delivered.

The overall conclusion to my process of deliverance would be the transformation of my mind. For me to stay delivered I would have to make the decision not to entangle myself again in the yolk of bondage. I realized that I deserved better and that if I wanted what God had for my life I couldn't compromise myself spiritually to have it. When I got free in my mind, then I got free in my body.

I had lost my spiritual identity by accepting the accusations and lies that Satan influenced this man to speak over my life. My life began to change when I became aware of what I allowed into all of my external gates, my eyes, ears and through what I spoke from my mouth. Death and life are in the power of the tongue and I had to speak life to uproot and destroy the things that died in my life through my involvement in that dead relationship.

Speak Life!

I had to be reconditioned in my mind spiritually so when I heard things spoken to me that were contrary to things that were of life and positive I would cast those imaginations down. You should not wait or ponder on the words that are spoken to you, cast those words down "immediately". This is the only way for those negative words not to take root in your thoughts.

Proverbs 18:21 (KJV)
21 Death and life are in the power of the tongue: and they that love it shall eat the fruit thereof.

2 Corinthians 10:5 (KJV)
5 Casting down imaginations, and every high thing that exalteth itself against the knowledge of God, and bringing into captivity every thought to the obedience of Christ;

You cannot become numb to someone insulting you. Confront the person that speaks those things to you by letting them know that you are not pleased with what they are speaking, and bring those negative thoughts captive to the obedience of Christ! I allowed them to take root in my mind and because of that those negative thoughts became a stronghold in my thinking that the enemy used to help with keeping me in bondage. I allowed someone to speak negatively to me, and I didn't realize that his words were what the enemy was using to attack my mind.

As I meditated on the Word of God my thoughts began to change and I got strong enough to fight against the attacks that Satan used to attack my mind. The weapons of our warfare are not in the natural but they are spiritual, so your fight must be a spiritual weapon which is the Word of God!

I had to learn to fight strategically through the Word of God. Binding and losing became power tools in my prayer life. There is a reason why the Lord said in that he would give you the keys of the Kingdom. Keys open things up. The Lord wanted me to know that as a servant of God that I could use the spiritual authority that He had given me by binding and loosing demonic spirits from operating negatively against my life. I had to study to get the revelation concerning those keys, but when I got revelation I activated my authority that God has given me to operate as an ambassador of the Kingdom of God.

Matthew 16:19 (KJV)
16 And I will give unto thee the keys of the kingdom of heaven: and whatsoever thou shalt bind on earth shall be bound in heaven: and whatsoever thou shalt loose on earth shall be loosed in heaven.

I made the decision to live a holy life. It's all about a decision. Freedom was a decision away for me and it's a decision away for you. If you are connected in a relationship that has caused you to lose sight of you then you need to evaluate this relationships value.

Emotional Ties

I went from having my emotions all over the place to becoming emotionally stable. Getting delivered from the emotional ties took prayer and fasting along with meditating on the Word of God. I had to transform my thinking so that my thoughts were not filled with the negative poison that I endured while being in that relationship. I went from living and walking comfortably in darkness to having the light of God covering all areas of my life. I didn't want to return to that situation so not visiting my past through those emotions was definitely a key to staying free. I would not return again to that vomit.

2 Peter 2:22 (KJV)
²² But it is happened unto them according to the true
proverb, the dog is turned to his own vomit again; and
the sow that was washed to her wallowing in the mire.

Once you get free you don't want to return again to the
bondage that you have been set free from. It's a choice and
I'm glad that I made the decision to stay free.

Galatians 5:1 (KJV)
¹ Stand fast therefore in the liberty wherewith Christ
hath made us free, and be not entangled again with
the yoke of bondage.

Severing all of my communication with this man
helped me as well to heal as my foggy thoughts cleared I had
a better perspective of what I had been through. Until you
heal emotionally you are not in a healthy state of being. I did
my own personal assessment that helped me to make the
final decision to walk away and not return again to the
relationship. It really feels good to be in a healthy place
emotionally. It feels like I have awakened from a deep sleep,
this is a place of mental clarity that I have not experienced
until this time in my life.

Soul Ties

1 Corinthians 6:16 (KJV)
¹⁶ What? know ye not that he which is joined to an
harlot is one body? for two, saith he, shall
be one flesh.

The breaking of the soul tie was the hardest part of
this battle. Breaking a soul tie means you have to let the
"Dr. Feel Good" Go! Stop it! Cut it off now! No more! That is
the way to your freedom. As long as you connect intimately
with this person you will be tied to them and you are open to
the same attacks they are open too. A major hindrance for
me and with me was that he was connected to spirits that
had been in him for a long time and now I was getting
attacks from them in my life.

This journey was not easy, but I believe my prior life experiences and hardships spiritually prepared me for this battle. I had to understand that the true enemy in this battle was not the man, but Satan's demonic forces. This man was the vessel that those spirits occupied to take out his devious plans to destroy my life. My testimony now is that "All things have worked together for my good".

Romans 8:28 (KJV)
[28] And we know that all things work together for good to them that love God, to them who are the called according to his purpose.

Another part of my victory came from me fighting back and not excepting the negative comments that were spoken to me and over my life on a consistent basis. You don't have to receive those reports. One of my favorite responses that I'm known for saying is that "I don't receive that", and I mean exactly that. I wasn't going to receive those comments and I spoke them directly to who was speaking those negative things to me.

I came out of this battle delivered, set-free and the spiritual wounds of my heart were healed from the emotional, mental and spiritual attack that the enemy of my soul devised against me. I have shared my journey and I pray that in some way you were blessed. I am alive again, but not just living. I'm alive in Jesus!

It is my heartfelt desire and the will of our heavenly Father to see you resurrected from all the dead things in your life that Satan has used to hold you captive. If you don't have a personal relationship with the Lord Jesus Christ; or if you are in a backslidden state, I would like to extend to you an invitation of salvation and rededication into the Kingdom of God.

God is waiting for you with outstretched arms and He wants you to know that He loves you very much. It was His love that rescued and delivered me and now He wants to rescue you. All it takes is a decision and you will be born again into the Kingdom of God and have a right that is given to His children. Love you to life!

Prayer of Salvation
(Pray this prayer out loud)

Heavenly Father, I come to you in the name of Jesus. I acknowledge to You that I am a sinner, and I am sorry for my sins and the life that I have lived; I need your forgiveness. I believe that your only begotten Son Jesus Christ shed His precious blood on the cross at Calvary and died for my sins, and I am now willing to turn from my sins. You said in Your Holy Word, Romans 10:9 that if we confess the Lord our God and believe in our hearts that God raised Jesus from the dead, I shall be saved. I confess Jesus as the Lord of my soul. With my heart, I believe that God raised Jesus from the dead. At this moment, I accept Jesus Christ as my own personal Savior and according to His Word, right now I am saved. Thank you, Father, for your unlimited grace which has saved me from my sins. I thank you, Father, that your grace never leads to condemnation, rather it always leads to repentance. Therefore, Father transform my life so that I may bring glory and honor to you alone and not to myself. Thank you, Father, in Jesus name I pray. Amen.

CHAPTER XIII

PRAYERS

Luke 18:1 (KJV)
¹⁸ And he spake a parable unto them to this end, that men ought always to pray, and not to faint;

Prayer doesn't just change some things, prayer changes everything. I encourage you to pray daily as it will build you up spiritually in the things of the Lord. It will also help you to develop a closer relationship with God because the more you are in His presence, the more you acquire your need for Him. He will give you revelation and understanding.

As you study the Word of God your prayers will intensify because you will have understanding on His promises and what is His will concerning things in your life. Be strong and of good courage, for the Lord still hears and answers prayer.

Breaking Soul Ties

Heavenly Father I come you in the name of Jesus asking for deliverance from every illegal soul tie that I have been connected to through fornication and illicit sexual acts. In the name of Jesus, I curse the soul tie of fornication and nail it to the cross of the Lord Jesus Christ.

I renounce and release every filthy word soul tie that has attached itself to my soul. I pray that the soul tie connection that I had with *(first, middle & last name of the person(s) and birth date if you know it. I repent of my disobedience and ask* for forgiveness. Cleanse me Father with the Blood of the Jesus Christ. Break every cord that has attached itself to my soul and I ask that your holy angels would severe those ties in the realm of the spirit.

 Allow your warring angels to fight against every principalities and demonic spirits that have attacked my life. I renounce every word covenant and vow that I have spoken that has allowed any soul tie to remain open in my life, I repent of it and ask for forgiveness for entering into those covenants. I ask that every portal or gateway that was opened through those soul ties be sealed shut with the Blood of Jesus. Father I ask that even the memory of those soul ties be erased from my mind and heart and that no residue of them shall remain in the name of Jesus.

Father in the name of Jesus I break every spiritual demonic soul tie that I have opened to the enemy, through masturbation and fantasy. I ask that every portal and gateway be sealed closed by the Blood of Jesus. I renounce those sins and ask for forgiveness from them. Father, cleanse me with the Blood of Jesus. I bind the spirits of the Incubus and Succubus that they will not enter into my dreams nor engage with my soul in any sexual act. I pray that if I have opened my soul up to them that they be cast back to the pits of hell in the name of Jesus.

Breaking Soul Ties
(continued)

Father, create in me a clean heart and renew a right spirit within me, cast me not away from thy presence and take not your Holy Spirit from me. I ask that my desire for holiness and purity would rise and that I will not entertain unholy things of this world. Father in the name of Jesus uproot even the soul tie of my past relationships and sever them from my soul in the name of Jesus. Father, I forgive anyone that I have had a soul tie with and I ask you to sever all alliances that I have had with them. Give me eyes to see any article that I have possession of that allows me to have an attachment to any soul tie, so that I may remove it from my life. In Jesus name, I cover myself in the blood of Jesus and I seal this prayer in the name of the Lord Jesus Christ. Amen

Deliverance

Heavenly Father, in Jesus name, I ask for your help in my time of need. I ask for forgiveness of my sins *(name those sins that come mind)*. *Father p*rotect me and deliver me from every evil spirit and evil influence that has been afflicting my life. I ask for wisdom and the power of your Holy Spirit to help me with this matter. Father, In Jesus name give me revelation concerning this situation. Teach me to war against the evil intrusion of the enemy and lead me into the victory through your precious son, Jesus Christ. Set me free from the power of sin, Satan and his kingdom of darkness. I plead the Blood of Jesus over my life right now, for I am redeemed by Jesus' blood, justified, cleansed and sanctified by the shed blood of Jesus Christ. I thank you that I have knowledge that the weapons of my warfare are not carnal but mighty through God to the bringing down of every stronghold. I come against the strongman of <u>manipulation</u> and I bind it with chains of irons and cast it back to the pits of Hell in Jesus name.

Father God in the name of Jesus I close up every portal and gateway to which demonic forces have had an entrance into my life. I seal those gateways closed with the Blood of Jesus. I renounce every illegal covenant word that I have spoken or that someone else has spoken over my live and I cancel them in the mighty name of Jesus. I repent of entering into these covenants and I ask for forgiveness for letting the enemy to enter into my life, Thank you for your grace and love. It is You, Lord, who always causes me to triumph in Christ Jesus, for your Word says, "you are able to do exceeding abundantly above all that I ask or think, according to the power that works in us. I choose to stand on your truth. I trust you and I believe your promises, In Jesus name I pray

Healing

Father in the name of Jesus I pray that you would heal me in my soul from the wounds of hurt and torment that was afflicted upon my life. I ask that you will forgive me of all my iniquities and heal all my diseases. I come against every lie that was spoken to curse my life and I decree and declare that no weapon formed against me shall prosper and every tongue that has risen against me in judgment you shall condemn. Health and healing is the children's bread and Father I enter into my covenant right for healing as your child.

Heavenly Father I ask that you send your ministering angels in healing in their wings to comfort me and to bring healing with them. I thank you Father that your promises are Yea and Amen and that there is nothing impossible to you. Every sickness and disease is subject to the name of Jesus, and in the name of Jesus I release healing over myself and I receive my healing in Jesus name. I pray that you heal my body from the physical manifestations of the attack of the enemy. Father, I ask you to restore me with a sound mind, spiritual deliverance and physical healing to take place in my even now Lord. For I trust you Father to do what your words have declared to me.

I give you praise and glory for all that you have done. I ask this prayer in Jesus name and I seal it with the Blood of Jesus in the name of Jesus. Amen

Clear Direction

Heavenly Father, In the name of Jesus Christ, I come boldly before Your throne of grace, seeking Your guidance and directions concerning my life. I pray that Your will be done in my life on earth as it is in Heaven. Father, please cleanse me of any worldly wisdom, any selfish motives, lust of the flesh, lust of my eyes, and pride of life, that may draw me away from Your purpose for my life. Lord count me worthy of Your calling, and by Your power may You fulfill every good purpose that you desire through my life.

Heavenly Father, I ask for wisdom regarding my predestined future, knowing that You give wisdom to everyone liberally and without reproach. I ask in faith, without doubting, expecting You to give me divine direction in every area of my life. I thank You in advance for the impartation of divine wisdom. Help me to be strong and of good courage as you lead me in the way that I should go. Father, give me the courage to follow the pathway of faith, not the path of fear, for you have not given me a spirit of fear, but of power, love and a sound mind.

I am trusting in Your word believing that You will not fail me or forsake me. Father, lead me in Thy path of righteousness, and go before me to make every crooked place straight. Search me O Lord and know my heart. Try me and know my thoughts and see if there is any wicked or hurtful way in me and lead me in the way everlasting. Father, lead me in Thy truth, and teach me: for Thou art the God of my salvation; on thee do I wait all the day. Lead me in a plain path so my enemies won't overtake me. Send out Thy light and Thy truth and allow them to lead and guide me in all that I do and all that I say.

Lord, you are my rock and my fortress. Show me favor and guide me in all my affairs. And when I cry out from my heart being overwhelmed, led me to the rock that is higher than I. Even in the midst of my storm let Your hand lead me, and Your right hand hold me. Instruct me in the way I should go and let Your eyes guide me. Teach me to do Thy will; for You are my God.

Lord, as I seek Your face I promise to trust in You with all my heart, lean not unto my own understanding. I will acknowledge You in everything that I do and allow You to direct my path so that I can always hear a word behind me saying, this is the way to go whenever I turn to the left or to the right. Lord, it is my desire to live a life pleasing to You and guided by the Holy Spirit all the days of my life. Father, please guide me continually and satisfy me so that even my dry seasons will be a watered garden with a spring of water whose waters never fail. Lord, guide me with Your counsel. For Lord, you are my Redeemer, the Holy One, the One who teaches me to profit and will lead me in the way to go.

Now Lord, I ask you to preserve my going out and my coming in from this time forth, and even for evermore.

In Jesus Name, Amen

Holiness

Heavenly Father you are the Holy One, you have called us to be holy, even as You are holy. Father reveal your Holiness to me, so that I will know Your Holiness and how I am to be holy. Cleanse me Lord from my iniquity and purge me with hyssop that I might be white as snow.

Show me how to enter into your Holy presence. Teach me to be a partaker of your Holiness. And when the sight of Thy Holiness only shows us the more how unholy we are, teach us that you make us partakers of your own Holiness those who come to Thee for it.

Father, we come to Thee, the Holy One. It is in knowing and finding and having Thyself, that the soul finds Holiness. We do beseech Thee, as we now come to Thee, establish it in the thoughts of our heart, that the one object of Thy calling us, and of our coming to Thee, is Holiness. Thou wouldst have us like Thyself, partakers of Thy Holiness. If ever our heart becomes afraid, as if it were too high, or rests content with a salvation less than Holiness, Blessed God! let us hear Thy voice calling again, be holy, I am holy. Let that call be our motive and our strength, because faithful is He that calleth, who also will do it. Let that call mark our standard and our path; oh! let our life be such as Thou art able to make it. Let now Thine own voice sound in the depths of my heart calling me, be holy, as I am holy. Amen.

www.ingramcontent.com/pod-product-compliance
Lightning Source LLC
LaVergne TN
LVHW091310080426
835510LV00007B/447